a handful of **herbs**

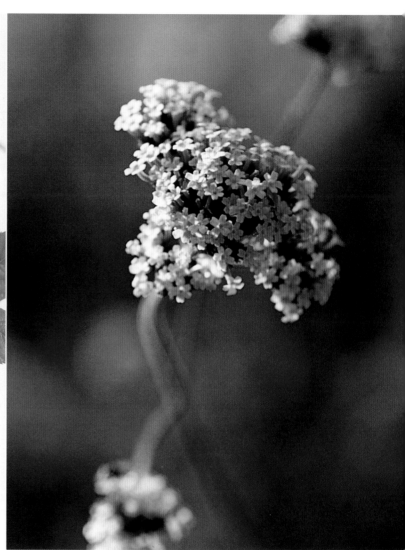

RYLAND
PETERS
& SMALL

LONDON  NEW YORK

Barbara Segall   Louise Pickford   Rose Hammick

# a handful of herbs

inspiring ideas for gardening, cooking, and decorating your home with herbs

*with photography by Caroline Arber and William Lingwood*

First published in the USA in 2001
This paperback edition published in 2007
by Ryland Peters & Small, Inc.
519 Broadway
5th Floor
New York, NY 10012
www.rylandpeters.com
10 9 8 7 6 5 4 3

ISBN 978-1-84597-363-6

Text © Barbara Segall, Louise Pickford, and
Ryland Peters & Small 2001, 2007
Design, illustrations and photographs
© Ryland Peters & Small 2001, 2007
photograph page 41 b © Jonathan Buckley

The original edition of this book was cataloged as follows:
Library of Congress Cataloging-in-Publication Data
Segall, Barbara
  A handful of herbs : inspiring ideas for gardening, cooking,
  and decorating your home with herbs / Barbara Segall, Louise
  Pickford, Rose Hammick ; with photography by Caroline Arber
  and William Lingwood.
    p. cm.
  ISBN 1-84172-028-3
  1. Herbs. 2. Herb gardening. 3. Herbs--Utilization. 4. Cookery
  (Herbs) I. Pickford, Louise. II Hammick, Rose. III. Title.
  SB351.H5 S438 2001
  635'.7--dc21
                                    2001031777


Printed in China.

Essential oils should not be used undiluted nor taken
internally except on medical advice. No responsibility
for any problem arising from their use is accepted by
the authors or publisher.

# Contents

# introduction

Every one of us feels that our own garden is a particular paradise, but the herb garden has the edge on them all. There is nothing quite like the rush of sensual pleasure that comes from simply brushing against a lavender bush, or stepping across a thyme or chamomile path.

These attractions don't end in the garden. Herbs can be brought into the house to be used fresh in cooking, or dried, frozen, or otherwise preserved for later use. Some can be transformed into potpourri or used in other ways to perfume and decorate rooms, or to freshen drawers and clothes, while others fragrance baths or become simple, gentle cosmetics and lotions.

Gardeners of the past discovered, probably through trial and error, which plants were safe to use in food and for healing. Down the centuries, herbs and other useful plants have come into our lives courtesy of various waves of invaders, travelers, and soldiers. Herbs were first appreciated for their medicinal qualities. In Western history, the medicinal use of herbs dates from the first century A.D., when the Greek physician Dioscorides set out the healing properties of more than 500 plants in what was one of the first descriptive herbals, his *De Materia Medica*.

In the herb gardens of today, it is not uncommon to find the culinary, medicinal, and folkloric traditions of the past combined with a modern appreciation of attractive plant forms. Most herb gardens are now enjoyed for the power-packed aromatic leaves of herbs such as rosemary, sage, thyme, lovage, and chives, as well as for the simple but enchanting flowers and useful seeds that many herbs offer. It is this continuity of the past in our present homes that makes the bountiful summer harvest of these useful plants so evocative and especially satisfying.

If asked to define a herb, most people would say it is a plant used in cooking, but the true definition of the term is much wider. It includes trees, shrubs, biennials, annuals, and herbaceous perennials that have culinary, aromatic, medicinal, and cosmetic uses. In addition, many are excellent decorative garden plants. Some herbs are used for their foliage and flowers, others for their seeds or roots, and some for all four attributes.

Barbara Segall

LEFT **The deep pink blooms of an ornamental achillea bring a touch of flamboyance to an herb garden.**

super herbs

With an ancient record in folklore and medicinal history, basil is also a highly distinctive culinary herb, especially in Asian, French, and Italian cuisines.

## BASIL
*Ocimum basilicum*

Best used freshly picked, basil can also be frozen in leaf form or in homemade sauces. It combines well with tomatoes for a salad and is the main ingredient of pesto sauce for pasta. It adds piquancy to pizzas and to chicken and lamb dishes.

There are at least 13 different types of basil, varying in foliage, color, shape, texture, and aroma. Flavors range from anise to cinnamon and the sweet, spicy, clovelike scent of sweet basil. Basil can grow up to 18 in (45 cm).

*O. basilicum* 'Purpurascens' has purple leaves and pinkish flowers. *O. basilicum* 'Citriodorum' is lemon-scented with green leaves and white flowers. Anise-flavored basil has pale pink flowers and a strong taste of anise. The tiny leaves of Greek basil, which grows in the shape of a small bush, offer the fullest flavor.

Plant basil in an herb garden or in containers in late summer, when there is no danger of frost or severely cold weather. In the herb garden, grow it in a sheltered sunny site in light, well-drained soil. If it is grown in a container, basil should be kept well watered in dry conditions.

Basil has traditional uses as a digestive aid and a herbal tonic, as well as being used in aromatherapy.

Bay leaves were the foliage used in wreaths to garland winners and achievers in classical Greece and Rome.

## BAY
*Laurus nobilis*

Glossy dark-green bay leaves are part of the *bouquet garni*, the traditional herb bundle used to add flavor to meaty dishes. Bay is also a good flavoring for sweet dishes, particularly rice pudding and other milk desserts; its delicate spiciness can be best enjoyed if the milk is simmered gently with the bay leaf before the other ingredients are added.

An evergreen tree with shiny, aromatic, spicy leaves, small yellow flowers, and black berries, bay can grow to 40 ft (12 m), but is generally slow-growing, and in containers its height is controlled. It can be clipped into geometric shapes or grown as an elegant ornamental standard. Shaped bay trees in pots are useful in herb gardens as focal points to mark a meeting of paths or to emphasize a change of height.

Buy young plants and plant them in spring or fall in rich, well-drained soil. Although bay will tolerate light shade, it prefers full sun. Protect young plants and plants in containers from frost with straw bales, bubble wrap, or burlap windbreaks. Cut back any frost-damaged stems in spring. Pick leaves as needed throughout the year.

*L. nobilis* 'Aurea' has golden leaves and makes an attractive color contrast in the herb garden. *L. nobilis* 'Angustifolia,' the willowleaf bay, is also attractive as a container plant and in the garden.

Infusions made from bay leaves have been used to stimulate appetite or to aid digestion.

# CHAMOMILE
*Chamaemelum nobile*

This hardy evergreen perennial is distinguished by flowers that resemble daisies, finely cut foliage—and a perfume that takes your breath away. Chamomile is widely used in cosmetics, soothing skin creams, and other medications. Its dried flowers can be steeped in hot water to make a relaxing tisane, but it has no culinary uses. The creeping, non-flowering variety of chamomile tolerates light foot traffic, making it suitable for covering a short length of path or the ground under a bench.

Grow chamomile in light well-drained soil in full sun. It can reach 8 in (20 cm) in height. Chamomile paths should be kept weed-free or the weeds will overwhelm the chamomile plants, eventually destroying the fragrant pathway.

Non-flowering lawn chamomile, *C. nobile* 'Treneague,' which has fernlike leaves, is used to create scented lawns and paths. Upright chamomile, which has daisylike blooms, is grown in flowerbeds for its flowers, which can be used fresh or dried. The double-flowered form, *C. nobile* 'Flore Pleno,' is an attractive addition to the garden, and its flowers are used to make chamomile tea.

The flowers, single or double, of upright chamomile have medicinal and cosmetic uses in facial steam baths and hair rinses; they also bring a soothing and relaxing fragrance to a bath. Dried flowers and leaves of chamomile can be added to potpourri.

A pineapplelike scent floats in the air when the leaves are crushed underfoot or gently squeezed between the fingers.

# CHERVIL
*Anthriscus cerefolium*

A refreshing salad herb, chervil is also useful as a feathery and flavorful garnish. Its light taste combines well with eggs, poultry, and soft cheese. Although best used fresh, the leaves can be preserved by being frozen in ice-cube trays.

Chervil is highly prized in France, where it is often used in omelets and as a component of the traditional *fines herbes* mixture.

Chervil is a hardy annual with pretty fernlike leaves and small delicate white flowers in late summer. It grows to 12 in (30 cm), thriving in a shady site in light well-drained soil. If planted as an inter-row crop, chervil takes advantage of shade from other row-crop plants. It dislikes root disturbance, so sow it direct into the growing site. Water plants well or they will bolt, flowering and setting seed too quickly, and you will lose flavorful foliage. Pick the leaves through the summer.

Chervil plants can be grown indoors on a shady windowsill, but indoor plants will lack the vigor and flavor of plants grown outdoors. In mild climates, you can also sow seed in late summer for a winter crop, which will need some protection through the winter.

Rich in vitamins, chervil has traditionally been used as a treatment for digestive and circulatory disorders.

Chives (opposite page, left) bring a hint of onion to garnishes and salads, while cilantro (opposite page, right) adds piquancy to curry and other hot dishes.

## CHIVES and GARLIC CHIVES
*Allium schoenoprasum* and *A. tuberosum*

Chives have spiky green leaves and mauve flowers, while garlic chives, or Chinese chives, have garlic flavor in their strappy leaves and white starry flowers that appear in late summer. The chopped leaves of both types combine well with egg dishes and are useful for garnishes and in salads. Chives are also among the ingredients of the traditional *fines herbes* mixture.

With its attractive flowers and good foliage, this perennial fits well into the flower garden. It makes an informal edging for part of a vegetable garden and, if planted into spaces in paving, will eventually spread to make its own shapely patterns in the paving gaps.

The spiky leaves shoot from the underground mini-bulbs in spring. They grow to about 10 in (25 cm), but can be harvested once they are about 4 in (10 cm) above ground. Either pull leaves from the clump or cut off a handful with a pair of sharp scissors.

In late spring even spikier shoots carrying the flower buds start to appear. Chive flowers come in a range of pink-mauve tones, as well as in a new form that is green to white. The flower heads, made up of numerous tiny flowers, are also edible and look attractive in salads. They are at their juicy best just as the buds begin to open.

Chives grow well in containers, but will need extra attention to prevent them from drying out. Young plants can be kept on a windowsill or planted in the sunniest site in the garden.

Chives have a traditional medicinal use as an antibiotic and as an appetite stimulant and a digestive aid.

## CILANTRO
*Coriandrum sativum*

A strongly aromatic, short-lived annual, cilantro is grown for its seeds and for its deeply cut, parsleylike leaves that bring spice and flavor to desserts and meaty dishes alike. It bears a profusion of tiny white flowers. For the full effect of their flavor to be appreciated, cilantro leaves should be added toward the end of the cooking time.

The dainty pinkish-white flowers that appear from early summer are followed by beadlike seeds, which are used in baking cakes and cookies as well as in curries, chutneys, and pickles. The leaves are added to stews and salads or used as a garnish. Plants grow to a height of about 24 in (60 cm).

*C. s.* 'Morocco' is a good form for seed production, while *C. s.* 'Cilantro' produces abundant well-flavored foliage. There are forms of cilantro that are offered for seed production as well as those for leaf production.

Cilantro grows well in a sunny spot in light well-drained soil. It needs a long hot summer for best seed production. Sow seeds in spring in the growing site and cover them with a cloche until established. Young plants should be kept well-watered and free of weeds until they are established. Pick young leaves before the mature ferny leaves develop.

Seeds tend to fall before they can be harvested, so the flower heads need to be picked before the seeds are fully ripe. Cover the flower heads and store them in a warm, dry, airy place so the seeds can ripen. Store the seeds in an airtight jar.

A cleansing spiciness is dill's gift to fish, soups, and salads.

### DILL
*Anethum graveolens*

An excellent partner for fish in any form, hot or cold, dill is particularly renowned as an ingredient of the Scandinavian marinated-salmon dish gravadlax. Its fresh young leaves bring spice to salads, egg dishes, and soups. The seeds, together with the flower heads, are used in pickles, preserves, and chutney. They are tasty with rice and cabbage, or as a flavoring for bread. Ground dill seed is used in curries.

A hardy annual with aromatic feathery leaves and clusters of yellow flowers in midsummer, dill grows to between 2 ft (60 cm) and 5 ft (150 cm), depending on the variety. The seed needs well-drained soil, full sun, and a sheltered site. Sow in the herb garden in spring, once the soil has warmed up. Because dill grows tall, it is not ideal in containers, but containers can be useful for a first sowing.

Water seedlings and thin to 8 in (20 cm). If necessary, support plants with a light framework of twigs. Water regularly in dry seasons, or the plants will bolt and flower, and leaf harvest will be minimal. Pick leaves as needed when they are fresh and young.

Harvest seeds for culinary use before they ripen entirely on the plant. Cut the flower heads off the plant, put them in paper bags, and leave them to ripen in a warm dry place. When the seeds are dried, clean off the husks and store the seeds in airtight jars, ready for use.

Many seed companies differentiate between leaf and seed dill. *A. g.* 'Sari' is a variety grown for high yields of leaves with short stems. *A. g.* 'Herkules' is highly aromatic, while *A. g.* 'Dukat' is selected for its good leaf production. (All these varieties also produce good seeds.)

Dill is used to calm upset stomachs and to alleviate insomnia. Ground seeds are sometimes used as a substitute for salt.

Fennel's wispy foliage is one of the delights of a herb garden in spring.

## FENNEL
*Foeniculum vulgare*

Bright-green leaf shoots unfurl in spring from pale leaf sheaths in which they are tightly packed like small parcels, scentedwith an unmistakable aroma. Fennel is different from bulb fennel, which is grown as a vegetable. The leaves are a flavorful addition to salads and soups, and make a good garnish. Bronze and green fennel can be combined to make a topping for salads. Both types are good partners for fish dishes. The seeds are also used in cooking and to make teas or tisanes. The flower heads can be used in pickling, and the leaves for flavoring oils and vinegars.

Fennel is a hardy perennial grown for its finely cut aromatic leaves in spring and summer, and umbels of small yellow flowers in summer. It can grow to more than 6½ ft (2 m) and self-seeds—so be ruthless when you see fennel seedlings in spring. The ornamental quality of its foliage makes bronze fennel, *F. v.* 'Purpureum,' rewarding to grow. It has chocolate-brown feathery leaves, which contrast well with the green of ordinary fennel. The aroma is the same.

Grow fennel in a sunny site in rich, well-drained soil. Sow in the growing site in late spring, or in containers in a greenhouse for earlier germination. Either thin or transplant, leaving a space of 20 in (50 cm) between plants.

Pick fennel leaves as needed through the spring and summer. The seeds should be harvested in the fall when they are ripe. Divide established plants of common fennel in spring or fall. Try to segregate plantings of dill and fennel, or they will cross-pollinate.

Fennel has traditionally been used as a treatment for a wide variety of conditions, but it is now most closely associated with the prevention of obesity.

Individual cloves of garlic can be used whole or chopped, crushed, or roasted in their skins to flavor meat dishes, salads, salad dressings, and bread.

### GARLIC
*Allium sativum*

Several separate small cloves wrapped in a paper-thin skin that ranges in color from rose-mauve to white are the components of a garlic bulb. Bulbs bought fresh from French markets or home-grown have an unbeatable flavor. Garlic is the main ingredient of many typical Mediterranean sauces, such as aioli, and is also valued for its health-giving effects.

Garlic grows to 12 in (30 cm). It does best if grown in fertile well-drained soil in a sunny position. Planting times vary, but gardeners with cool or cold winters—below 68°F (20°C)—should plant individual cloves in fall, in rows 12 in (30 cm) apart. Keep them well watered, especially in dry periods.

Lift bulbs in summer when the foliage has yellowed. Leave the bulbs on racks or in wooden boxes to dry for a day or two in good weather, then hang them up in bunches in a dry, airy shed.

There are several different varieties of garlic available, with varying strengths of flavor; bulb and clove sizes also vary. *A. sativum* has white flowers, while *A. scorodoprasum* (also called rocambole) has a mild-flavored bulb as well as edible bulbils mixed with flowers on its flower heads. Elephant garlic, *A. ampeloprasum*—which has a huge single onionlike bulb—is sometimes available at supermarkets. Buy several bulbs, some to use and some to plant for next year's crop.

Traditionally used in the treatment of many conditions, garlic has been shown to lower blood pressure slightly and to boost the body's immunity to infections; it also has antiseptic qualities.

Long valued for its cleansing properties, and associated with fresh-smelling linen, lavender takes its name from the Latin for "to wash."

## LAVENDER
*Lavandula* species

Lavender flowers can be used in baking and jam-making or to flavor sugar. More often, the dried flowers and foliage are used to perfume rooms or packed into sachets and hung in closets. Flowers destined for potpourri or for making into lavender bottles or bunches should be harvested as soon as they open, when the color and aroma are at their most intense.

With gray-green, softly textured, highly aromatic leaves and (depending on species and variety) deep-blue, purple, white, or pink flowers, this evergreen shrub grows up to 40 in (1 m). It thrives in a sunny, open site in well-drained, slightly sandy soil. *L. angustifolia* 'Hidcote,' which has a uniform, compact shape and produces very deep-blue flowers, is a good choice for edging a path or small bed. There are also forms with green, white or red flowers. Some lavenders, including *L. stoechas* and wooly lavender, *L. lanata*, are less hardy and need winter protection.

Lavender is useful as an edging or a hedging plant for a path or small parterre. Provided that you use plants of the same species or variety, the uniformity of shape and color make it useful in formal as well as informal situations. It tolerates clipping into a variety of shapes. Cut back any woody stems in the fall and remove old flower heads left on the plant from the previous season's flowering. Sow fresh seed in late summer or fall. Transplant seedlings to 24 in (60 cm) apart or 12 in (30 cm) if growing as a hedge. Take cuttings in summer.

Lavender has been used therapeutically for its calming effects, as well as in the production of cosmetics and perfumes.

## LEMON BALM
*Melissa officinalis*

A powerful lemon scent, released when its leaves are brushed against, and a fresh zesty flavor help to tip the balance in favor of lemon balm, despite the fact that it can become invasive in a small garden. It grows in soft mounded shapes that suit the front of a bed. Leaves of lemon balm give a strong citrus flavor to salads.

Lemon balm is a hardy perennial, growing to 40 in (1 m) when in flower. Its rather insignificant flowers are carried on untidy-looking stems from midsummer to fall. Lemon balm can be useful for areas in the shade, as long as it is planted in well-drained but moist soil.

*M. officinalis* has plain green leaves. *M. o.* 'Aurea' is a golden-and-green variegated form that is very useful for introducing bold splashes of color to the herb garden. *M. o.* 'All Gold' has yellow foliage.

The variegated form of lemon balm in particular combines well with other plants, but its flower stems should be snipped off to encourage leaf production. Once the flowers have formed, the variegation tends to deteriorate.

Cut back flowering stems in the late fall to contain the plant's tendency to self-seed. Pick leaves when required for fresh use and to dry or freeze. Sow seed in spring and divide established plants in fall or spring.

A few leaves of fresh lemon balm in boiled water make a tasty tea, which has traditionally been used to relieve the symptoms of stress and tension.

To make the most effective herbal tea, harvest lemon balm before it comes into flower, when the essential oils are at their strongest.

Often reaching 6½ ft (2 m), lovage has a height and stature that make it useful as a tall accent plant at the center of an herb garden.

## LOVAGE
*Levisticum officinale*

**Lovage has a strong spicy flavor and a long history in traditional English cooking. Its foliage slightly resembles that of celery.**

A hardy perennial with large dark-green leaves, lovage can grow up to a height of 6½ ft (2 m). Clusters of small pale-ocher flowers, resembling those of parsley, appear in late summer. It does best in a sunny site in rich well-drained soil. Plants should be watered regularly until established.

Lovage looks attractive near angelica, and if grown at the base of a rose will hide the rose's bare stems. Divide plants in spring or fall every two or three years. Pick leaves when they are needed and seeds when they are ripe.

Lovage adds spiciness to food. Fresh leaves and stalks can be sprinkled into soups and stews for a meaty flavor, or blanched and eaten as a vegetable. Young leaves are delicious in salads and make an elegant garnish for main dishes. Seeds are sometimes added to cookies before baking. They can be crushed and used as an ingredient of mixed-herb marinades, and are valued as a remedy for digestive complaints.

Every herb garden should have at least one type of mint. With aromas and flavors for all occasions, mints also have much to offer in the shape of ornamental leaves and flowers.

## MINT
*Mentha* species

Chop mint into vinegar and mix it with sugar and a little warm water to make mint sauce, the natural accompaniment for roast lamb. Mint jelly, made with apples and mint, is also satisfying with lamb dishes. In Middle Eastern countries mint is used in cooked and cold food, as well as in drinks such as mint tea.

The genus *Mentha* includes some 25 species of perennials grown for their leaves, which are usually oval to lance-shaped and toothed at the edges. The ornamental flowers, ranging from deep mauve to light pinkish-lavender in color, attract bees and butterflies.

Mint thrives in full sun in well-drained but moist soil. Set young plants out in spring or fall, and divide clumps that are growing in the ground in the fall. Mint will grow equally well in light shade and, as long as there is a source of water, provides good ground cover. To restrict its rapid sprawling growth, plant mint in a deep plastic or tin container, and sink the container into the ground.

Gingermint (*Mentha* x *gracilis* 'Variegata') has a spicy flavor and green leaves splashed with yellow. Pineapple mint (*M. suaveolens* 'Variegata') has wooly-textured green leaves, marked irregularly with creamy white, usually at the margins. Spearmint (*M. spicata*) and peppermint (*M.* x *piperita*)—both vigorous, spreading plants with attractive flowers—have the flavor traditionally associated with mint. Probably the most highly scented variety is lemon or eau-de-Cologne mint (*M.* x *piperita* 'Citrata'), which has a bronze tone in its leaves and stems. The perfume of its leaves is overwhelming if it is eaten, so it is better enjoyed as an aromatic foliage plant.

Mint is at its most aromatic before it comes into flower, so cut it back to encourage leaf production. Harvest the leaves through the growing season—they can be used fresh, or dried or frozen for later use. Mint may succumb to mint rust, which shows as rusty markings on the leaves. Remove affected plants and burn them, sterilize the soil, and replant with new healthy plants in another part of the yard.

## OREGANO or MARJORAM
*Origanum* species

Oregano and wild marjoram are two names for *Origanum vulgare*, whose spicy aromatic leaves add zest to many meat and tomato dishes, and are an indispensable ingredient in Greek and Italian cuisines. The herb's various types of foliage and flowers also provide subtle ornament in the herb garden.

There are many other species of marjoram belonging to the *Origanum* genus, the more decorative of which can be used as edging plants or in mixed beds, where their attractive flower stems and aromatic leaves can be readily enjoyed. Some marjorams, including sweet marjoram (*O. majorana*), are half-hardy or tender—either grow them as annuals or protect them in winter.

Golden marjoram (*O. v.* 'Aureum') and gold-tipped marjoram (*O. v.* 'Gold Tip') provide wonderful splashes of color in an herb garden. Golden marjoram has clusters of pretty tubular flowers in summer. Its foliage is a lemony-golden color and makes a good display in the herb garden—but it should be planted in a semishady site to avoid leaf scorch from the sun. Gold-tipped marjoram has green leaves tipped with gold, and needs to be grown in a site that is not too shady or it will lose the variegation.

Compact marjoram (*O. v.* 'Compactum') grows to 6 in (15 cm), with a spread of 12 in (30 cm), and makes a good ground-covering mat of foliage. Pot marjoram grows up to 18 in (45 cm) and is propagated from cuttings.

Of the several different forms of oregano or marjoram that can be used in cooking, the best are Greek oregano (*O. v.* subsp. *hirtum*) and pot marjoram (*O. onites*). Some, including *O.* 'Kent Beauty' and *O. laevigatum* 'Herrenhausen,' are generally regarded as decorative plants in the herb garden rather than for culinary use.

Oregano or marjoram does not need pruning as such, only the cutting back of flowering stems in late summer and of all stems to ground level in the fall.

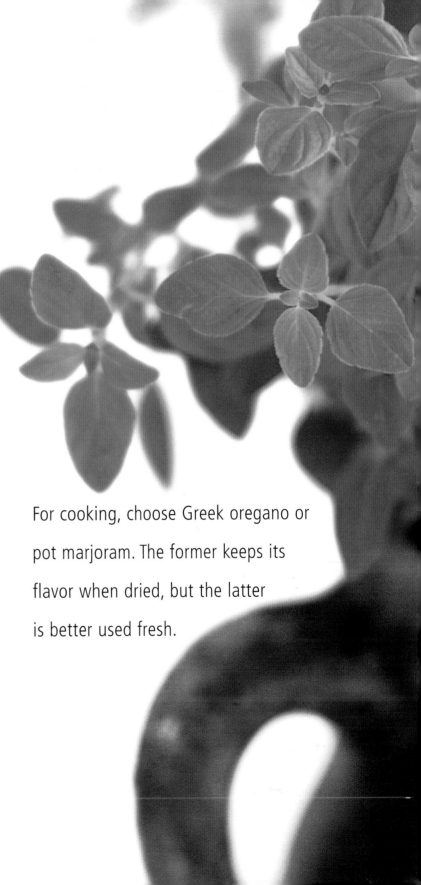

For cooking, choose Greek oregano or pot marjoram. The former keeps its flavor when dried, but the latter is better used fresh.

Part of the traditional *bouquet garni,* parsley (opposite page, left) is also a popular garnish, while rosemary (opposite page, right) is a classic partner for lamb.

## PARSLEY
*Petroselinum crispum*

A basic herb of many cuisines, parsley is one of the main components of the *bouquet garni* herb bundle. You can use the leaves chopped up or whole in salads, as a garnish or as a flavoring for sauces and soups.

There are several varieties of curly-leaved parsley, with tightly curled mosslike leaves. All grow as low compact plants during their first year and flower in their second year. Also attractive, but much larger, is flat-leaved parsley—*P. c.* 'Italian,' or Italian or French parsley. It grows to a height of 12 in (30 cm). Its foliage is flat, and the stems and leaves are delicious either in salads or in cooked dishes.

Parsley is a hardy biennial that needs to be handled gently when it is transplanted because root disturbance will trigger its survival mechanism and set it in flowering mode too early. It prefers moisture-rich soil and partial shade. Buy plants in spring or fall. Cover fall-planted parsley with fleece or a cloche in winter to ensure a good supply of fresh herb.

The chopped leaves of parsley freeze well, and whole leaves can be dried for winter use. You can use parsley to make an alternative to Italian pesto sauce (usually made with basil), for parsley butter, and in homemade cosmetics.

It is said that chewing parsley after drinking alcohol or eating garlic freshens the breath.

## ROSEMARY
*Rosmarinus officinalis*

The delicate flowers and strongly aromatic leaves of rosemary are ornamental in the herb garden and have long been valued as ingredients in cooking, herbal cosmetics, and traditional remedies. The leaves can be dried or frozen for later use.

Rosemary has spiky aromatic leaves on woody branches. It is a hardy evergreen perennial in most areas, but may need protection in harsh winters. Upright forms can reach 6½ ft (2 m), and the prostrate form spreads and trails. Harvest from growing tips to keep the plant bushy and encourage foliage production. Rosemary flowers in summer, with, depending on species and variety, small aromatic blooms in pink, white, or blue.

*R. o.* 'Prostratus' is a tender trailing or prostrate form with blue flowers. *R. o.* 'Albus' is hardy and has white flowers. For a tall rosemary hedge, choose *R. o.* 'Miss Jessopp's Upright'. 'Silver Spires' is a rediscovered old rosemary that was popular in Tudor times; it has silvery variegated leaves and is attractive in any season. 'Majorcan Pink' is half hardy and has pink flowers, while *R. o. lavandulaceus* is tender with blue flowers. *R. o.* 'Sudbury Blue' has delicate deep-blue flowers.

This herb prefers a sunny site with a little protection from cold winter winds. Good drainage is essential. Remove any stems that die back in cold weather, and cut back the plant to keep it in shape after flowering. Take cuttings in summer. Pick leaves when needed, but remember that the aromatic flavors are at their best before flowering. Whole stems or sprigs can be dried or frozen for later use. For drying in bulk, harvest in late summer.

Use rosemary flowers and chopped young leaves in salads. Sprigs of rosemary can be laid on cuts of meat before baking; the leaves are added to herb butters, jams, jellies, and summer drinks, and are used to flavor sugar for desserts. Rosemary salt is good for seasoning meat and marinades. The herb is an ingredient of some homemade and commercial skin cleansers and hair conditioners.

# SAGE
*Salvia officinalis*

Sage has been grown as a medicinal and culinary plant since ancient times. The name Salvia comes from the Latin word *salvere*, meaning to heal or save, and common sage—known for its astringent qualities—has been widely used as an antiseptic and cleansing herb in remedies and cosmetic preparations. Gargling with an infusion of sage can help relieve sore throat pain.

A hardy evergreen shrub with aromatic and decorative leaves, sage is as versatile in the kitchen as it is ornamental in the flower garden. It is used in numerous meat dishes, sometimes mixed with onion, and in salads, as well as in flavoring salt, oil, and vinegar.

There are many sages that look decorative in flower beds, including *S. o.* 'Tricolor' with leaves variegated in purple, pink, and white. Common sage has grayish-green leaves. Purple or red sage (*S. o.* 'Purpurascens') has purple-gray leaves, while golden sage (*S. o.* 'Icterina') has golden-green leaves.

Sages like full sun, an open site, and light, well-drained soil. Replace plants that become too woody. Take cuttings in spring or mid-fall, or layer branches *in situ*. Common sage and its varieties can be grown from seed, sown direct into the growing site when danger of frost has passed or in seed trays, cells, or plugs, where temperatures of 60–70°F (16–21°C) will ensure germination after two or three weeks.

If you are growing sage primarily for its useful leaves, cut out the flowering stems; pick leaves whenever you need them for cooking.

The classic herb for pork dishes, sage is often combined with applesauce to form one of the best-known partnerships in English cuisine.

# SORREL and BUCKLER LEAF SORREL
*Rumex acetosa* and *Rumex scutatus*

Sharp and clean to the taste, sorrel is an often undervalued element of the herb garden. Made into a sauce, it is a refreshing accompaniment to oily fish and adds piquancy to casseroles and stews. Buckler leaf sorrel (pictured), which has a milder taste, is particularly good in salads or as an alternative to spinach.

One of the traditional herbs of French cuisine, sorrel is an herbaceous perennial that, once established, will be in the herb garden forever. It dies down in winter, but in spring its fresh green leaves appear—and at that time are at their tangy best for use in salads or sauces.

There are two sorrels that are useful in the kitchen and the garden. Common sorrel or garden sorrel (*R. acetosa*) is a strong-growing herb that makes large clumps of shield-shaped leaves, which should be eaten before the plant flowers; tall stems shoot up from the leaf mounds in summer, and the leaves on these stems do not taste as good. Small, unremarkable blooms are carried at the ends of the branched flower stems.

Of greater attraction in the garden is buckler leaf sorrel or French sorrel (*R. scutatus*). This comes in a green form and a more interesting silver-variegated form, 'Silver Shield,' which has a marbled silvery center to the leaf and gives good ground cover.

Sorrel is valued mainly for its culinary attributes and has been used to treat blood disorders. It has a high oxalic acid content and, if consumed in large quantities, may be harmful, especially to the kidneys—so use with caution.

Sorrel is one of the unsung treasures of the herb garden, especially when included in a sauce to serve with oily fish. Its tangy leaves can also be chewed to relieve thirst.

Tarragon packs a powerful punch in its narrow lancelike leaves. Often teamed with chicken, it is also the herb used to make *sauce béarnaise*.

## TARRAGON
*Artemisia dracunculus*

The fiery anise flavor of tarragon makes it perfect for spicing meat and fish dishes. The leaves also add piquancy to oils and vinegars, and are excellent in marinades. Pick the leaves during spring and summer to use fresh, and in late summer to freeze for winter use.

French tarragon is a half-hardy perennial with narrow, pale, greenish-gray leaves. It can grow to a height of 60 in (1.5 m) and in summer produces insignificant flowers that never reach maturity. This means that tarragon does not produce viable seed, so it can be propagated only by using root or stem cuttings.

Grow tarragon in light well-drained soil in a sunny site, and cut it back in the fall. Protect the crown with a covering of pine needles or straw during winter. Divide plants in spring or fall.

There is a less tasty but more vigorous form of the herb called Russian tarragon (*A. dracunculoides*), which is often sold wrongly labeled as French tarragon. This species is very hardy and will survive winters without protection, but it is worth growing French tarragon for its flavor, which is far superior to that of the Russian variety.

Although it has no modern medicinal uses, tarragon was once valued as an antidote to snakebite.

# THYME
## *Thymus vulgaris*

An evergreen that can be used freshly picked all through the year, thyme is a component of *bouquet garni*. Both the flowers and the leaves are good in salads and are used to flavor oils, vinegars, and marinades, as well as soups and stews. Thyme is commonly added to stuffing for chickens. It combines particularly well with rosemary.

Thyme is a hardy evergreen subshrub with small, powerfully aromatic, spike-shaped, or round leaves. There are variegated silver and golden forms.

The most vigorous and most useful for basic flavoring is common thyme (*T. vulgaris*), which has deep-green leaves and is a many-branched woody subshrub. It has mauve flowers. *T. v.* 'Silver Posie' has silver variegated leaves and good flavor. *T.* x *citriodorus* is a shrubby thyme, with small green lemon-scented leaves and pink flowers.

*T.* x *citriodorus* 'Silver Queen' is variegated with creamy silvery leaves, rosy-pink buds and a strong lemon scent to its leaves. *T. serpyllum* 'Snowdrift' is a creeping thyme that carpets the ground in white when in flower.

The herb is versatile enough to be grown in the garden, in rock gardens, or in containers. The low-growing forms can be used to make attractive flowering paths or fragrant mats at the feet of benches. On a patio, plant cracks in or gaps between paving to make aromatic stepping stones.

Grow thyme in full sun in well-drained soil. After flowering, cut back the plant to promote new growth and bushy shapes. Replace plants every few years, when they become too woody and open at their centers.

Thyme has a traditionally been used as an antiseptic.

Both upright and creeping forms of thyme produce aromatic leaves and attractive clusters of small pink, mauve, or white flowers, which are as useful as the foliage in flavoring food.

# gardening with herbs

# how to grow herbs

Herbs are versatile plants that grow well in most types of garden soil and in most conditions. Their numbers can be increased by dividing plants or taking cuttings. Seed can often be sown where the plants are to grow, also known as "direct sowing." Or you can sow it in pots or seed-starting units, growing the seedlings on a sunny windowsill, under lights or in a greenhouse. Direct-sow the seed of hardy annuals in spring, either in a seedbed or in their growing sites. Half-hardy herbs can also be sown in their growing sites once all danger of frost has passed. Sow the seed in rows and just cover it with soil; water in well and thin out when the seedlings are well established.

Sowing indoors produces plants ready for planting out as soon as the soil warms up and the seedlings have been hardened off in spring. Almost fill seed trays or pre-formed seed-starting units with soil, firm the surface down, and water the soil, or stand the trays in water. Leave the trays to drain before sowing fine seed into the soil surface. Space out large seeds and sift a thin covering of soil over them.

LEFT  **Use sharp clean scissors to harvest herb flowers such as those of lavender. Cut low down on the stem, so that you have long stems to tie into bundles for drying. Harvest on dry days, when the sun has just burned off the dew and before it gets too hot. Lay the harvested material in a basket and keep it in the shade until you are ready to use it. Harvest only the amount that you can work with in a short time, or the flowers may begin to deteriorate and wilt.**

SEQUENCE STARTING FROM FAR LEFT **Put a label in place before you sow. Empty the seed packet into your hand and then take a pinch of seed, or one seed if they are large, and place it in a trench or hole. Barely cover the soil and firm it down with the back of your hand. Mark the line of the row with a trail of colored gravel, especially if you are sowing parsley, which is notoriously slow to germinate. Keep in mind that some seed requires light to germinate and should not be covered.**

Some types of seed will benefit from bottom heat. Use a heat mat or propagation unit for improved germination. Once the seeds have germinated and are large enough to handle, transplant them into small individual pots. Harden off the seedlings by leaving them outside during the day and returning them to the greenhouse at night, until they are acclimatized to outdoor conditions. In addition, be sure to increase the exposure to sun gradually.

Before buying an herb that is ready to plant in the yard, check for disease or pest problems; avoid plants that are root-bound or have damaged stems. Plant the herb as soon as possible, but not during the hottest part of the day. Dig a hole large enough to take the rootball, and remove any weeds from the soil. Put the plant in the hole, backfill with soil, then firm the surface of the soil and water the plant well. In dry conditions water the plant daily until it is well established.

Evergreen herbs such as bay, rosemary, sage, and thyme can be harvested from outdoor and indoor herb collections all year around, as can herbs that you have forced into growth in winter, such as mint, tarragon, and chives. Annual herbs, including basil, perilla, rocket, dill, nasturtium, and coriander, are at their best in spring and summer— late summer in the case of basil. Because herbaceous perennial herbs including fennel, lovage, and comfrey die back in winter, their harvest period is during the spring and summer. When each plant has produced good leafy growth, harvest it in an even way, to maintain a well-defined shape. For a handful of leaves to add to salads or cooked dishes, pick the herbs just before you want them, at any time of day.

To promote the vigorous growth of your perennial herbs or to increase their numbers, divide the plants in early spring when they are still dormant, or in the fall when the growing season is coming to an end. In the fall, before dividing, cut back all the old flowering stems. Then use a fork to pry the clump out of the ground. When it is loosened, lift it out and place it on the soil surface.

The traditional way to divide large plants is to place two forks back to back in the center of the clump and pry the two sections of the plant apart. Do this until you have reduced the size of the original clump and produced several new sections ready for replanting. Herbs such as chives can be pried apart by hand. Most perennials, such as marjoram, chives, echinacea, tarragon, sorrel, creeping thyme, and lovage, grow to form large basal clumps. The growth at the center becomes weak, and leaf production usually declines. When the clump is divided, any unhealthy-looking sections can be discarded, which allows the new plant or division to grow healthy new shoots from the rootstock around its edge.

By taking cuttings from individual plants, you can produce many new plants for your herb garden. You can use a cutting to reproduce exactly the plant from which you have taken the cutting.

As soon as the herbs begin to grow in spring, look for strong and healthy new shoots to use as cutting material—these are called softwood cuttings. Cut them away from the parent plant with a sharp knife, and if you are taking several cuttings, put them in a plastic bag to keep them moist and cool, and to prevent them from wilting.

Prepare several pots or trays with a good, well-drained seed-starting mix. Make a clean cut on the stem of each cutting just below a leaf node, so each is 4 in (10 cm) long. Cut the lower leaves off each cutting, but leave a few leaves on the stem. Make holes in the soil with a dibble, and put the cuttings in the holes up to the level of the remaining leaves. Label each cutting with name and date, then put the pot of cuttings in a heated propagator or a mini-greenhouse made with a plastic bag. Check the cuttings daily; if you are using a plastic bag, take it off and turn it inside out every day When roots start to appear on the underside of the pot—between two and four weeks—you can begin to apply liquid fertilizer. When the plants are large enough, pot in larger pots. Pinch out the growing tips of leafy shoots to encourage a bushy habit.

The method for taking hardwood cuttings is similar to that for taking softwood ones, but hardwood cuttings prefer very well-drained soil, and since they are taken later in the year—in the fall, when the stems are hard and woody—they need to be overwintered in cold frames or greenhouses before they can be planted out the following fall. The rooting time for hardwood cuttings is much longer than for softwood cuttings.

SEQUENCE ON RIGHT **Unless they are in a very large and congested clump, chives can easily be divided by hand. Dig up and divide the clump into smaller sections by gently pulling it apart. Discard dead or damaged material. Replant smaller sections in prepared planting holes. Backfill and firm in soil at the surface. Trim the tops of the newly divided plants and water them. Keep the row weed-free and in a short time you will have a crop of fresh chives.**

A simple way to propagate or increase herbs is to take root cuttings in spring or fall from healthy-looking plants. Mint, bergamot, lemon balm, horseradish, comfrey, and sweet woodruff are among the herb plants that can be increased this way.

Unless they are grown in crowded situations where there is no free circulation of air, or the plants are kept either too wet or too dry, herbs usually remain free of pests and diseases. It is preferable to use organic methods instead of commercial insecticides or fungicides to deter pests from food plants such as herbs. Many organic gardeners use insecticidal soap to get rid of whitefly or greenfly infestations. Brown spots on mint and chive foliage are

symptoms of a disease called mint or onion rust. Plants that are badly affected should be dug up and removed from the bed, so that other plants are not infected. You can also sterilize the soil around mint plants to prevent this disease from occurring: Place a layer of straw around the affected plant and set the straw on fire—but take care to make sure the fire does not spread.

Seedlings of basil and other herbs are prone to damping off and dying in the early stages of growth. Deterrents include good air circulation, hygienic conditions, judicious watering, and drenching the soil with a fungicidal compound before sowing.

Scale insects may be a problem on the evergreen leaves of bay grown in containers indoors. Use a soapy liquid to wipe the leaves, and dislodge the scale insects with the end of a cotton swab.

Vine weevil, whitefly, and red spider mites may be persistent in protected environments, but can be controlled with insecticidal soap or biological controls. Eelworms or nematodes are used for vine weevil, a parasitic wasp called *Encarsia formosa* for whitefly, and *Phytoseiulus persimilis* for red spider mites.

## Many herbs self-seed abundantly. Others can be increased by dividing clumps, taking cuttings, or sowing fresh seed in spring.

# beautiful beds

Many of the plants categorized as herbs are attractive flowering or foliage plants that can be taken out of the context of the herb garden and used successfully in a mixed bed. Sage—whose foliage colors range from silver to purple, and include a tricolor variety that is gray-green with hints of pink and white—is a particularly effective bedding plant. It grows to form a low mass of colored foliage, so it can be useful at the base of plants such as roses, which may have bare stems. Later in the season, when it flowers itself, sage offers extra ornament. Once the flowers have faded, cut back the plant to prevent it from becoming leggy and out of shape and to encourage continuous foliage production.

If you have space to accommodate their invasive habits, herbs such as mint, comfrey, and sweet cicely will provide good-textured, colorful, and shapely foliage followed by pretty flowers. All three are useful in shady sites, with mint being suited to moister conditions. Borage is another vigorous but useful foliage plant that bears eye-catching blue or white flowers in summer.

Johnny-jump-ups, with their small mauve "faces," are useful in containers as well as at the front of a bed, winding their way through other plants. Their silver foliage and dainty pink or white scented blooms make pinks suitable for low-growing at the front of the bed. Similarly, thyme will provide variegated gold or silver foliage, delicate white, mauve, or pink blooms and, in some cases, a low-growing habit.

Oregano or marjoram is a rewarding herb for the middle or front of a flower bed, and will grow to form fairly large clumps of flowering stems in white or mauve.

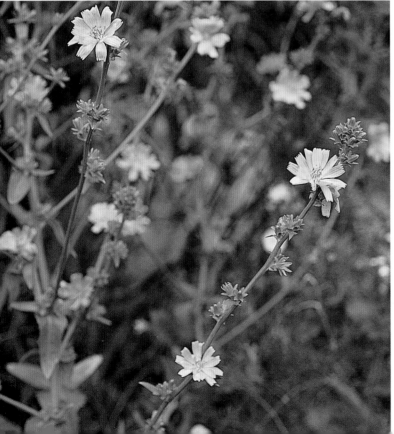

ABOVE LEFT **Mauve marjoram graces the front of a bed, while evening primrose, chicory, and fennel offer tall stems of flowers in yellow and blue, white, or (in some species of chicory) pink, which seem to float high in the air.**

BELOW LEFT **Starlike blue chicory looks lovely** en masse**, as well as in a mixed planting.**
RIGHT **Curry plant and lavender grow in curved shapes, which makes their silver-gray foliage useful for softening the edges of beds.**

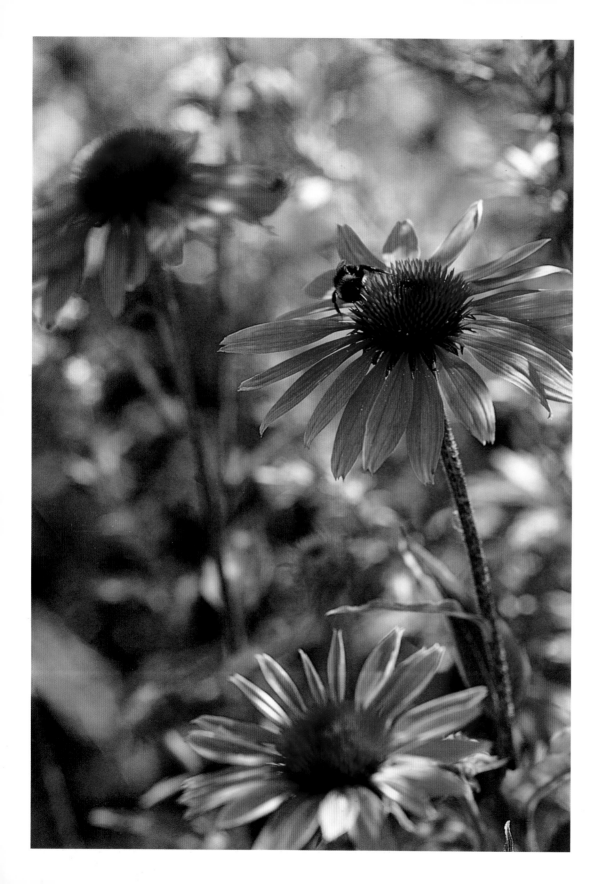

LEFT **Echinacea, or purple coneflower, is a native American herb with a long medicinal tradition. It has many potential uses in modern medicine, and is constantly being assessed for its potential benefits to the human immune system. In the flower bed, it offers attractive long-lasting blooms late in the season.**

OPPOSITE PAGE, ABOVE
**Boxwood trained into formal shapes is a useful accent in a mixed bed. Marjoram and bee balm, or monarda, bring a lovely combination of foliage and flowers to the bed.**

OPPOSITE PAGE, BELOW
**Calendula, or pot marigolds, will brighten a sunny bed in spring and early summer. To encourage continued flowering, remove the old flowers before they set seed.**

Most herb flowers are in the mauve, pink, or white ranges, but plants such as fennel, calendula, with its sunny orange and creamy yellow flowers, and nasturtium, in shades of orange, cream, and red, provide great swaths of color in the mixed bed. Nasturtiums have the added advantage of colorful foliage and look good weaving their way along the front of the bed. St. John's wort can be used to add spots of buttery yellow to the front of a bed, complementing evening primrose in a similar shade at the back; both herbs will self-seed copiously, so cut them back once the blooms are finished.

At a slightly higher level, fennel's early offering to the bed is a froth of ferny foliage in either green or bronze, followed by stiff upside-down umbrellalike flower heads with masses of small yellow dotlike flowers. These are a magnet for beneficial garden insects such as hoverflies, and because fennel self-seeds abundantly around the garden, at the height of summer it offers great stands of color, seemingly dancing with life.

Lavender, pinks, and some other herbs grow in soft mounded shapes that spill over the edge of the bed. Others, such as chicory, offer flowering stems that seem to float through other plants in the bed. Rosemary and bay are useful grown as standards in formal gardens, serving to raise eye-level and to make a repeated theme along a long bed.

In late summer, traditional herb-garden plants, such as echinacea, or purple coneflower (also available in a white and a green form), are especially useful because they flower over a long period late in the season. Bee balm, or monarda, has a similarly long and late flowering season, and provides tall stems of flowers arranged in whorls of mauve, white, and pink around its square stems. Hyssop, with mauve-and-white flower spikes, is also useful for the middle of the late-summer bed.

# covering the ground

Many low-growing herbs can be effective in the ornamental garden as groundcovering plants. Creeping thyme, for example, makes a flat green mat of foliage, and in summer offers its small mauve blooms for extra show. In a bed it hugs the ground at the feet of taller plants, suppressing weeds and providing its own color. Deadhead thyme after flowering, using shears or clippers. Remove any weed seedlings that grow through the groundcover and water it in dry spells.

Since it supports light foot traffic, thyme can be used for a short path. More formally, it makes a witty and attractive feature planted in a circle at the base of a sundial. You can also use a slightly taller variety for an inner circle within the creeping thyme outer circle, adding contrast to the color and texture of the groundcover.

Creeping chamomile is also useful as a fragrant groundcover, to create an aromatic lawn or as a path plant. Remove all perennial weeds and any stones from the soil before planting. For 1 square yard (1 square meter), you will need 40 individual chamomile plants. Water the plants in well, and avoid walking on the path or lawn until they are well established and have meshed together.

Either thyme or chamomile makes a fragrant cover for a grass seat or bench. Site the seat against an existing wall and make a back for it with trellis or wood. You can build up the seat in front of it as you would a raised bed, using smaller raised beds to form the "arms" of the seat. Plant the creeping herbs in the soil within the various raised areas and, if you are using trellis for the back, plant a climber such as jasmine into the bed, for fragrance in the air and at your back.

Prostrate rosemary, although it is slower growing than thyme and chamomile, and also tender in cold areas, is effective both as a groundcover and trailing over the edges of beds. Plant in full sun.

Corsican mint, *Mentha requienii*, won't support feet, but it does make a good cover at the edge of a pond or in a moist, shady conditions. Similarly, creeping mint, *M. pulegium*, is attractive in a shady, slightly damp area of the yard. Herbs such as *Alchemilla mollis*, sweet cicely, and salad burnet, although not ground-hugging, are useful groundcover plants in a large yard. They self-seed abundantly, so their spread can be prodigious.

LEFT  Two types of thyme form the groundcover that frames pots holding lemon verbena and an ornamental garden plant, Perovskia 'Blue Spire.'

ABOVE AND RIGHT  Creeping thyme (above) or chamomile (right) wears better when grown between stepping stones. Either herb supports light traffic and provides an aromatic path to a bench or an arbor. Both need clipping back to stop them from covering the stepping stones.

# a hedge of herbs

Rosemary, thyme, santolina, boxwood, and lavender are among the herbs that can be grown as shaped low hedges to enclose formal features or even to form the fabric of herb parterres. Herb hedges are usually shaped to make linear ribbons of foliage that outline or emphasize special areas of a herb garden. Yew may be slow-growing, but once it is established, it is a very elegant dark-green foil for herbs, and it is particularly useful as an architectural hedge plant.

Knot gardens and parterres are the usual formal features created with herb plants. The color of the hedge depends on the plants you choose for it. For a silvery effect, use lavender or santolina or even curry plant. Thyme, rosemary, and boxwood provide green elements, and by mixing the silver and greens you can create a woven effect.

Although you can achieve a formal effect by keeping lavender closely clipped, you can also create a relaxed and informal look by

OPPOSITE PAGE **A circle of wall germander, or _Teucrium chamaedrys_, is created from single plants of the same size planted in a particular design, then cut back annually to form the desired shape.**

RIGHT **Cotton lavender or santolina can be grown to achieve a silvery effect.**

BELOW LEFT **After it has finished flowering, cut back the lavender to a uniform height for a fragrant hedge.**

letting it flower in summer, then cutting it back once the flowering is finished. A lavender hedge makes an attractive feature on each side of a path, but remember to make the area wide enough to allow the lavender spikes to spill across it while leaving enough space for you to walk along.

In a vegetable garden use parsley, wild strawberries, or chives to edge part of the garden. This will provide an informal and semi-permanent hedge, which will alter as you harvest from it.

When you plant an herb hedge, use plants of the same height and size so you achieve a uniform look more quickly. Plant boxwood or yew in individual planting holes along a line of string. Water the plants in well and, if necessary, provide a temporary windbreak of burlap to help young plants survive their first winter.

When the hedge is well established, you can begin to clip it to maintain it. Cut back knot-garden or parterre hedges in the early fall, so there is time for them to recover before the cold weather sets in. Woody plants such as sage, thyme, lavender, and rosemary should be cut back to half the year's growth to promote bushy shapes. For extra effect, cut special shapes, such as triangles, globes, or even whimsical animals or birds, into the hedges.

# herbs in the vegetable garden

Growing popular culinary herbs such as parsley and chives as crops in the vegetable garden means you can harvest from several plants at the same time rather than from one or two—so each plant loses some of its foliage, flowers, or seeds, but enough remains for the plant to continue to be decorative and viable.

Group tall-growing plants such as fennel and lovage together and plant them at the back of the vegetable garden so they don't cast shade or take light away from lower-growing herbs. Low-growing herbs such as parsley, salad burnet, chives, and buckler leaf sorrel look attractive in short rows in raised beds.

Sow parsley in succession through the summer so you have a number of rows at different stages. Once parsley begins to send up a strong, tough flowering stem its foliage becomes less aromatic, and you should uproot the plants. If you have an informal vegetable garden, allow one plant to flower and set seed, and then to self-seed.

Summer savory, an annual with tasty edible flowers and foliage, has traditionally been cooked and served with beans; it is also often used as a companion plant for beans in the vegetable garden. Another good companion herb is sweet cicely, traditionally linked with one of the early fruits of the productive garden, rhubarb. Use its leafy shoots to sweeten and reduce the acidity of rhubarb. Sweet cicely self-sows copiously, so remove its seeds once they have formed or harvest them to use as anise-flavored sweets.

Mint is an invaluable kitchen herb, useful in salads and in cooked dishes, sauces, and jams and jellies. It is a vigorous plant, and is best grown in containers sunk into the ground, or in a section of the vegetable garden that can be cordoned off from the rest of the rows. Although its flowers are attractive, keep cutting out flowering stems to encourage more leafy shoots.

Cut back thyme and sage after flowering to promote the growth of new leafy shoots. Rosemary also benefits from cutting back. Some woody herbs become leggy and unshapely in time. If this happens, replace them with new plants.

Grow golden marjoram and chervil in relative shade in the vegetable garden. Chervil is a biennial producing leafy growth in its first year, so make successive sowings to keep your kitchen supplied with its subtle flavors.

Herbs such as nasturtium, johnny-jump-ups, and calendula provide edible flowers for use in salads. Chive flower heads are also good in salads—pick them just as the buds begin to open.

OPPOSITE PAGE, TOP ROW
**Confine vigorous mint (left) in a restricted area of the vegetable garden. Rosemary (center) can be clipped into shapes or allowed to grow freely. Use flat-leaved parsley (right) as a seasonal edging.**

OPPOSITE PAGE, BOTTOM ROW
**Harvest the aromatic seeds of caraway (left) after the flowers die back. Mossy curly-leaved parsley (center) can also be used as a temporary edging. The flowers, foliage, and seeds of nasturtiums (right) are spicy in food – and it will romp through the vegetable garden, providing annual color.**

Shrubby herbs such as rosemary, sage, and thyme need extra space in the vegetable garden, but you are unlikely to need more than one or two of each to support your cooking needs.

# creating an herb collection

If you have space to grow herbs for ornament, display them in groups according to their use or to show the differences between plants in the same genus. There are herbs for every theme and color scheme. For example, collections of mint, rosemary, thyme, sage, lavender, and marjoram reveal a wide range of foliage color, flower color and, in many cases, essential oils and aromas. Such collections, arranged by genus and species, show the characteristics of the various plants and display the differences between each species and form.

Before you plant a collection, you need to know the maximum heights and spreads of the various plants and how much sun they need. Look at the different foliage colors and place them so they look good together.

The simplest collection consists of the herbs you use often in the kitchen. Grow them in a small circular bed or in containers close to the kitchen door for easy access. You could devote a small rectangular bed to bay, thyme, and parsley, the three classic herbs of a *bouquet*

ABOVE **Mints are best grown in individual pots to prevent these vigorous plants from overwhelming each other.**

LEFT **Rosemary flowers can be white, pink, mauve, or blue. Most species are medium-height, but 'Miss Jessopp's Upright,' which can grow to 8 ft (2.5 m), needs to be carefully sited in such a collection, as does prostrate or creeping rosemary.**

RIGHT AND OPPOSITE PAGE **A circle is a popular shape for a basic culinary collection containing herbs such as rosemary, chives, marjoram, and buckler leaf sorrel.**

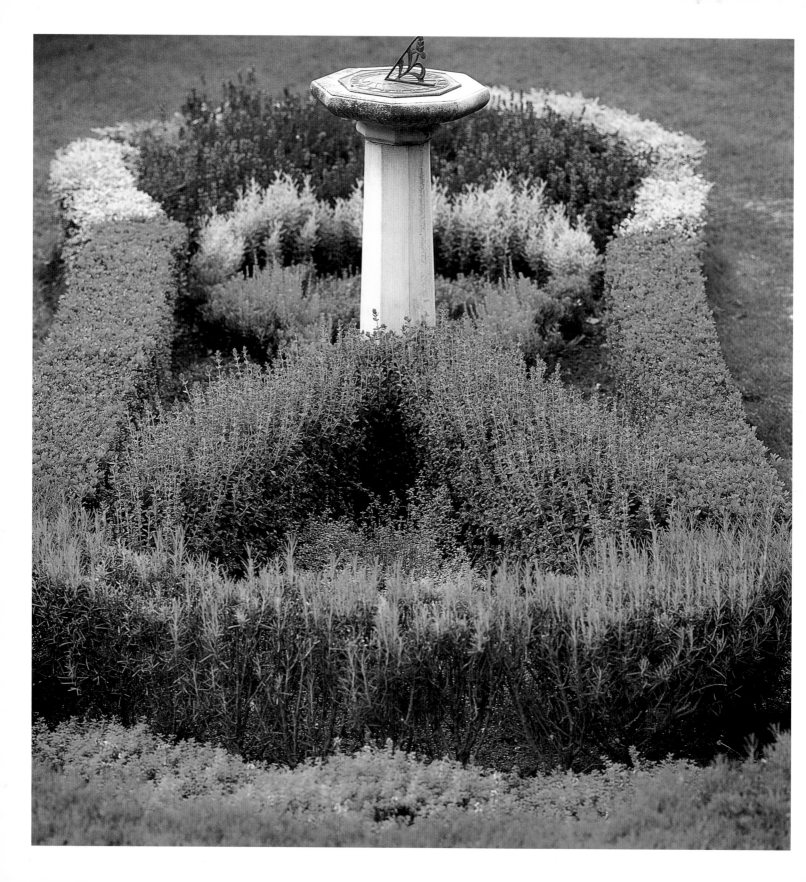

*garni*. Choose a standard or conical-shaped bay as the central focus. Plant thyme in the corners of the bed, and fill the center with parsley. For a *fines herbes* collection, grow parsley, chervil, chives, and tarragon. If you like Italian cuisine, grow bay, basil, marjoram, garlic, rosemary, and sage. For an Asian taste, choose coriander, lemongrass, mitsuba, perilla, and mint. Pizza herb gardens containing marjoram, basil, basil, and rosemary are also popular.

You could also group together herbs whose leaves are used dried or fresh to make teas and tisanes, such as sage, mint, bergamot, and chamomile. Other possibilities include fragrant herbs for a potpourri collection, and an edible flower collection. Enjoy cowslip and violet flowers crystallized or baked in cakes and scones. Use calendula, chive, and thyme flowers fresh in salads. Lavender flowers and rose petals added to ordinary or superfine sugar will transform it into a scented sweetener for baking and desserts.

The many herbs that have citrus-scented foliage would make an attractive collection with their differing heights, shapes, foliage, and flower colors. Such plants include variegated lemon balm, lemon verbena, lemon thyme, and some tender herbs such as lemon-scented basil, lemongrass, and lemon-scented gum.

LEFT **A number of different thyme species are grown within a small parterre or knot garden, hedged in by rosemary, box, and a golden form of the honeysuckle Lonicera nitida, 'Baggessen's Gold,' a shrubby hedge plant.**

RIGHT **Edging an informal path with collections of marjoram and catmint offers a flowing, curving shape to the garden and displays differences in flower color.**

# herbs in containers

Many low-growing or trailing herbs grow well in containers, and using containers makes it simple to replace old herbs quickly as particular plants reach the end of their productive life or as different varieties become available during the course of the season.

The most convenient containers for kitchen herbs are windowboxes placed just outside the kitchen—so you can harvest foliage and flowers easily and quickly without having to step outside—or large ground-level containers on a patio.

If any of the herbs in a container dies, or you harvest them so completely that they are no longer attractive, it is simple to remove and replace them. In addition, if you are going to be using and replacing the herbs regularly, you can leave them in their individual containers, all set into a sturdy wooden windowbox, with the box becoming a cachepot for the various smaller containers. You can replace any herb that is not growing well without having to replant the whole box.

There is a range of different containers that are suitable for herb growing. Terra cotta and plastic are popular choices, but you can use almost anything, from large olive-oil cans to half-barrels, to create a particular style and house your herb collection.

There are two things you need to be sure of when planting a container with herbs. First, it should have a depth of at least 10–12 in (25–30 cm), to give the roots plenty of space to make strong root runs. Second, larger containers are heavy to move once they are full of moist soil, so you need to put them in an appropriate location

LEFT **Terra cotta pots are attractive containers for herbs because they weather so well. Annual herbs and some perennials, including chives, thrive in small pots in the short term. Woody perennials such as sage and thyme need relatively deep pots so their roots can get properly established.**

before you plant. If you are planting a windowbox or hanging basket, make sure it is anchored securely in position. When it is full of moist soil it will be very heavy, and if it became unsecured, it could fall and hurt someone passing underneath it, especially if you happen to live in an apartment.

Remove the individual herbs from their nursery pots and place them on a drainage layer of broken terra cotta and a layer of potting soil. Fill the spaces between the herbs with soil and firm the plants in with your hands. Water the soil and cover its surface with a layer of grit to hold the soil in place and to act as a mulch.

There are a number of herbs that will thrive growing together in a container in a sunny situation. Avoid tall-growing plants—especially for a windowbox where the window opens out—because they will flop over the edge and may be damaged by wind.

## Low-growing or trailing herbs and stately standards make a fine display in containers.

ABOVE **Thyme and sage combine well in a basket with ornamental flowering plants such as trailing verbena.**
BELOW AND BELOW RIGHT **Weathered stone sinks or sculpted terra cotta** pots are practical and attractive containers for shrubby herbs such as sage. They are also suitable for low-growing collections of creeping and upright thymes.

LEFT **Standard bay trees make strong focal points in a formal herb garden. In winter, insulate the pot with bubble wrap to prevent frost damage and stablize it so it doesn't blow over.**

OPPOSITE PAGE **A bold and flamboyant display in a container can be used as a marker for the meeting point of paths or to provide a change of height in a low-growing herb garden.**

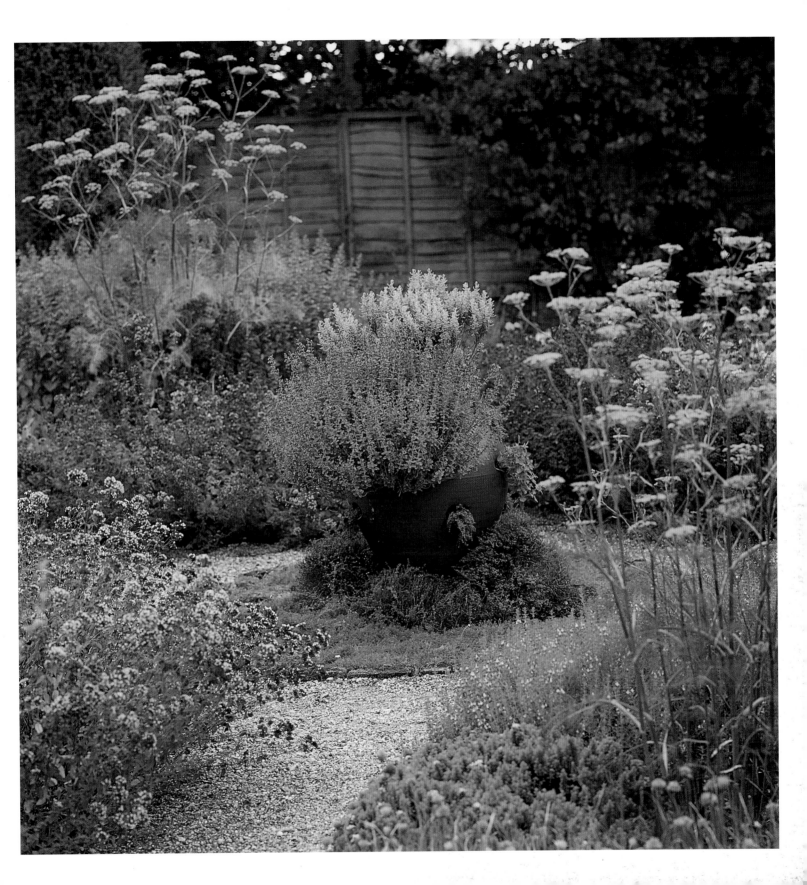

# growing herbs indoors

Many herbs can be grown indoors all year around, but indoor herbs are especially useful in winter for quick harvesting. In sheltered sites they can also be grown on patios and balconies throughout winter.

It is advisable to treat indoor herbs as practical or useful plants with short shelf or windowsill lives rather than as long-lived plants. Like other container-grown plants, they need nutrients, water, protection from pests, adequate light, and free circulation of air.

A kitchen windowsill is usually the most suitable site for herbs in pots because it is convenient for the cook and is likely to have good light and air circulation. Choose attractive containers for an extra decorative effect, or group several herbs in larger containers to create a mini-herb garden indoors.

As a general rule, herbs should be grown in separate pots in well-drained soil. This allows easy replacement of dead or over-harvested herbs. Water the plants regularly, but in winter keep rosemary, sage, winter savory, and thyme just moist.

Herbs grown indoors in summer need a liquid feed every two to three weeks—or add a slow-release granular fertilizer to the soil when you pot the plants. Use a spray of insecticidal soap to kill off aphids; spray every 14 days until the infestation has abated.

Harvest from the herbs as required, but turn each plant every few days to encourage even leaf growth and to help you harvest evenly from it. If you over-harvest from one plant it will look less attractive and may become more vulnerable to pests and diseases.

For quick results, replace indoor plants with new ones bought from supermarkets; for a longer growing period, replace them with herbs from garden centers. You can sow parsley and chervil in succession to provide new material.

Evergreen herbs, such as rosemary, sage, and thyme, grow well indoors. Annuals such as basil and parsley last for a short time, but replacement pots can be bought regularly from supermarkets for immediate use.

If you have no garden and are growing herbs in pots indoors all year around, repot evergreen perennials annually in spring. The plants may need replacing every two or three years. Plants such as fennel

# Supermarkets can be a good source of unusual culinary herbs for growing indoors.

and dill, which would normally grow very tall outdoors, should be harvested when they are reasonably short, or the plant will become leggy and look untidy and out of line with its windowsill companions.

If you have a heated greenhouse, you can force tarragon, mint, and chives into growing during what is normally their dormant season. Pot them in the fall and keep them in the greenhouse through the winter, planting them in the yard in spring.

Container herbs can be bought from many supermarkets at any time of the year to fill the flavor gap between your own sowings and provide leaves for salads and cooked dishes. The hothouse conditions in which they are grown are difficult to replicate in the average drafty kitchen, but you can prolong their lives by keeping them out of drafts, watering them from the base and harvesting them evenly. Even if you are careful with them, it is unlikely that supermarket plants will become long-term inhabitants of your indoor collection. In some circles they are known as "cut-and-chuck" herbs because of their short-term use.

Supermarkets can also be a source of unusual herbs for indoors. For example, lemongrass plants can be grown from stems bought in supermarket packs. (In some Asian supermarkets, they are sold loose.) Choose the plumpest stem and check that it has not been sliced at the base. Plant the stem in gritty soil and keep it on the dry side during winter. Alternatively, good-sized plants are available from specialized herb growers and will provide citrus-scented foliage much earlier than the supermarket stems.

LEFT **Fennel, parsley, basil, and sage will grow well on a sunny windowsill, but they need to be kept out of drafts. Fennel tends to become leggy if it is grown indoors in a container, so use it quickly.**

living with herbs

To create a warm welcome, bring the essence of a summer garden indoors with a potpourri of flowers, herbs, and spices.

The original "rotten pot" that gave us the word potpourri was a wet mixture of fermented petals and leaves. Today, the dry potpourri is more popular. Its scent may not last as long as that of the moist variety, but the combinations of textures, colors, and aromas are endless. The basic ingredients are flowers for scent or color, aromatic leaves, peel, and spices, and a fixative—usually powdered orris root—to preserve the blend. Use 1 tablespoon of orris root for each cupped handful of dried flowers and leaves; then add a few drops of essential oils, if desired.

ABOVE AND OPPOSITE PAGE **For a zesty hallway, add essential oils of bergamot, grapefruit, and lemon to a bowl of dried lemon balm, lemon verbena, mint, yellow rosebuds, and citrus slices. Any essential oil must be used sparingly or it will drown the subtler scents of the leaves and petals. The potpourri in this shallow bowl—about the size of a dinner plate—needs no more than 2 drops of each oil.**

RIGHT **To enhance the rustic feeling in a room with plenty of wooden furniture, mix 2 or 3 drops of essential oils of pine, sandalwood, and cedar with large handfuls of dried rose petals, bay leaves, and lavender sprigs, along with generous sprinklings of ground cinnamon and nutmeg.**

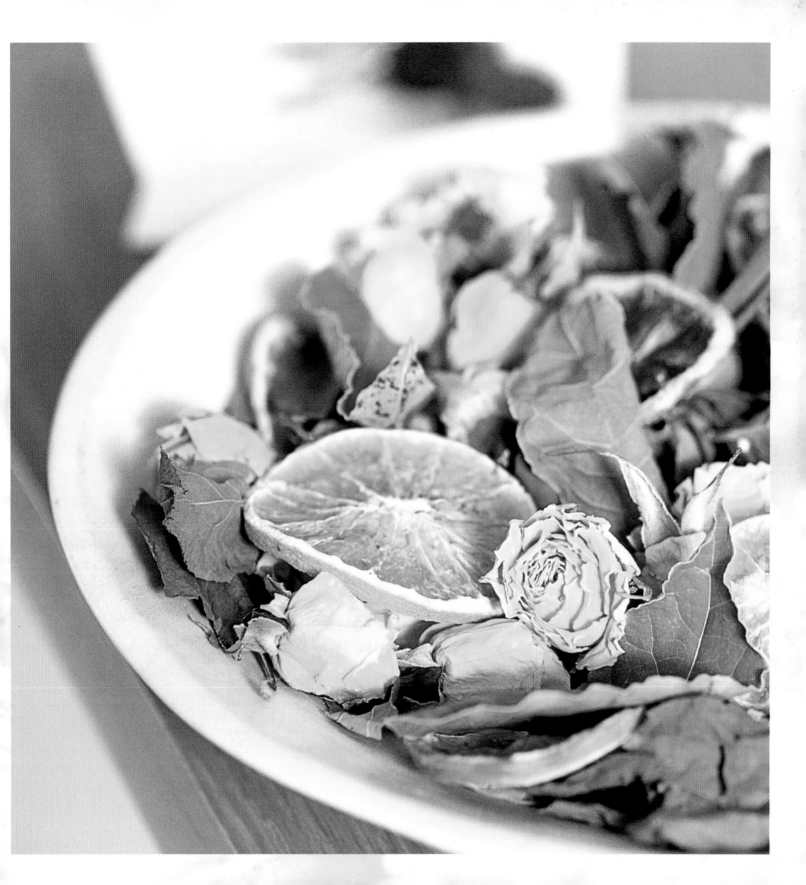

Designed for comfort and entertaining, living rooms are full of textiles and display surfaces that offer a host of opportunities for scenting and decorating with herbs.

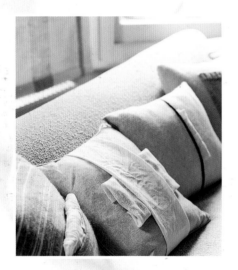

A simple way to scent your home is to have arrangements of fresh flowers and herbs in every room, but there are other, more imaginative ways to keep it smelling delicious and inviting all year round.

For example, herb sachets—which have traditionally been used to freshen drawers and linen cupboards—can also be tucked into pillows, into the pockets of everyday coats and clothes, and down the sides of comfy chairs and sofas. Fragrances are released when herb-filled cushions are pressed or leaned against; curtain hems can be filled with dried aromatic herbs, or fresh lavender sprigs can simply be tucked into voile curtains. Experiment with different mixtures of dried herbs and essential oils to make a potpourri, perhaps combining it with a pomander. Circulating air will pick up and mingle these scents, so make sure the various fragrances are complementary, and there is no clash of pungent odors.

For a sweet aroma, choose from herbs that sweeten, which include bay, lavender, lemon verbena, rosemary, santolina, myrtle, thyme, and sweet woodruff.

ABOVE LEFT AND OPPOSITE PAGE **Herb sachets can be a decorative element in themselves, while subtly perfuming an entire room—the perfect setting in which to enjoy a cup of chamomile tea.**

ABOVE RIGHT **For a heady, long-lasting winter fragrance, press cloves into oranges to make pomanders. Display several in a dish with a selection of herbs and spices such as bay, eucalyptus, juniper berries, and cinnamon.**

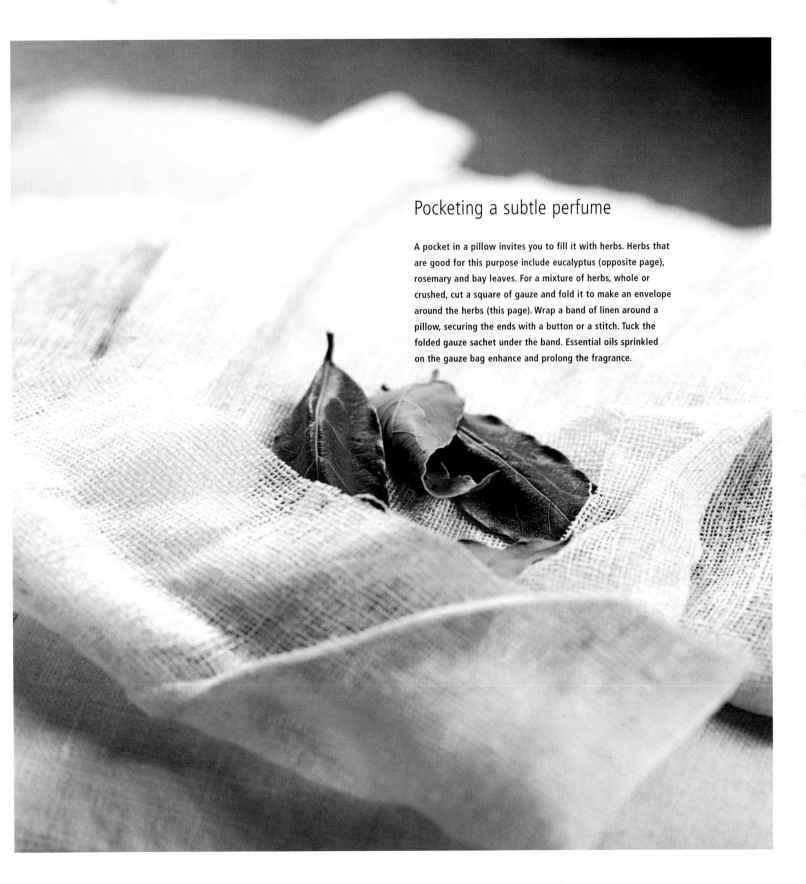

## Pocketing a subtle perfume

A pocket in a pillow invites you to fill it with herbs. Herbs that are good for this purpose include eucalyptus (opposite page), rosemary and bay leaves. For a mixture of herbs, whole or crushed, cut a square of gauze and fold it to make an envelope around the herbs (this page). Wrap a band of linen around a pillow, securing the ends with a button or a stitch. Tuck the folded gauze sachet under the band. Essential oils sprinkled on the gauze bag enhance and prolong the fragrance.

A handful of woody sprigs on a log fire intensifies the smoky aromas of winter.

ABOVE AND LEFT If you have a log fire, throw on a handful of woody-stemmed herbs every so often to release the rich aromas. Layering logs with branches of rosemary both looks pretty and complements the woody smells.

Burning woody herbs such as rosemary, lavender, and bay will fill a room with rich musty aromas. Either keep a box of dried herbs by an open fire to use as kindling, or throw an occasional handful on the embers. Layer logs stored in the home with generous sprigs of rosemary (drying the rosemary beforehand should stop it from turning black).

Another delicious winter fragrance is the smell of burning candles. To create your own herbal version, buy a candlemaking kit. Just before pouring the melted wax into molds, add small pieces of dried herb, such as bergamot, wall germander, lavender heads, lemon thyme, mint, rosemary, or myrtle, or a few drops of essential oil of your choice.

# A flamboyant winter wreath creates a Yuletide mood.

One of the most traditional ways of using herbs for decoration is to weave them into a wreath. This adds fragrance and color to a room and, if used imaginatively, can become the central focus. The wreath shown is a strong enough statement to be the only festive decoration in the room.

To make a wreath, use plain wire, moss-covered wire, or willow, and secure into a hoop. (Or buy a hoop ready-made from a florist.) Using thin wire, attach bunches of selected herbs. For the main body of the wreath, use branches of pine, rosemary, eucalyptus, and bay; then carefully tuck in among the branches slices of dried oranges, lemons and limes, fresh or dried Chinese lanterns, and bundles of cinnamon sticks. For the final festive touch, add bunches of red berries.

If the wreath is to hang horizontally, attach it to a strong structure such as the iron candelabra illustrated. When it is time to take the wreath down, burn the bunches of herbs on an open fire and enjoy the powerful aroma.

LEFT AND RIGHT **A wreath of pine branches, eucalyptus, rosemary, bay, slices of dried citrus fruit, and bundles of cinnamon sticks will fill a room with a distinctively festive mixture of colors, textures, and fragrances.**

Generous bunches of dried herbs, or herbs preserved in attractive bottles of oil or vinegar, can be used in the kitchen for decorative as well as culinary purposes.

The medieval still room for processing and preserving herbs has long since disappeared from the home. Such activities are now likely to take place in the kitchen, where herbs may also be stored, grown (see pages 54–55), or—as in other rooms—used decoratively.

As soon as possible after harvesting or buying herbs, put them in water and out of direct sunlight. To revive cooking herbs that are starting to wilt, put them in a plastic bag filled with air and secure it tightly; stored in the refrigerator, they should last a few extra days.

The sooner after harvesting the drying process begins, the better the quality and color of the dried herbs, but drying cannot be rushed because moisture must be removed gradually from a plant. Wipe off any soil or grit, but avoid washing the leaves. Choose a warm, dry,

dark place with good ventilation, such as a heated attic. Hang several sprigs of each herb in separate small bunches, tied loosely with string or raffia, so the air can get in and around each bunch. Leave herbs hanging, stems upward, for about a week, until the leaves are paper-dry and fragile, but not disintegrating. Remove leaves from stems, keeping them whole, and store in airtight bottles away from sunlight.

Check dried leaves regularly for moisture, mold, and insects, and throw them away if you find anything wrong. Most dried herbs will last for about a year.

Freezing is a good way to retain the color and flavor of delicate herbs such as basil, chives, dill, and tarragon. Before freezing, wipe the herbs and pack them into labelled plastic food bags or boxes.

ABOVE LEFT  **To dry herbs, tie a few sprigs together and hang them in a warm, dark room.**
ABOVE  **Herb oils and vinegars should be stored in airtight bottles out of direct sunlight.**

RIGHT  **Hanging herbs from the ceiling can produce a dramatic decorative effect. Bunches of sage, lemon balm, rosemary, and eucalyptus, dried or fresh, will brighten up any kitchen.**

RIGHT The acrid smell of rue repels flies and ants. Hang up bunches of the herb in utility rooms to discourage infestations, and press the leaves occasionally to release their pungent scent.

BELOW Pretty posies of santolina in your linen drawers will ward off the dreaded moth.

LEFT **To give a wonderfully fresh fragrance to floors and surfaces, clean them with 6 drops of an essential oil added to a quart (2 litres) of warm water. Choose from oils of lemon, lavender, tea tree, thyme, sandalwood, peppermint, and eucalyptus.**

RIGHT **To make your wooden furniture smell dreamy, add a few drops of essential oil of lavender to good-quality beeswax furniture polish, and apply with a clean dry cloth.**

Herbs have always had an important practical role in the household, and that remains true today—indeed, incorporating herbs or essential herbal oils in your cleaning routine can make household chores an aromatic pleasure. You can use them to disinfect floors and surfaces, to repel unwanted visitors such as moths and other insects, and to sweeten and purify stale, musty air.

Ants are seen off by sprigs of pennyroyal, rue, and tansy left on pantry shelves. Rue also deters flies, as do lavender, mint, mugwort, pennyroyal, and peppermint. Use the herbs dried in potpourri, or fresh in arrangements and wreaths. Disturb the leaves occasionally to release more scent. To prevent unwelcome visits from weevils, place a few bay leaves in canisters of flour, rice, and dried legumes.

Herbal preparations have a multitude of practical uses in the home—and they are frequently kinder to your skin and the environment than chemical-based cleaners.

ABOVE **Roses, pelargoniums, and Chinese lanterns add color to a summer garland of flat-leaved parsley, bay, lemon balm, coriander, fennel, apple mint, eucalyptus, and sage.**

RIGHT **In addition to making flamboyant centerpieces, fresh herbs can be used for plate decorations, in finger bowls, and in place-marker pots.**

FAR RIGHT **Leaves of borage and mint with cucumber slices make iced water even more refreshing. Coriander flowers impart a delicate flavor to pepper and salt.**

Decorating a summer table with fresh herbs is a joy in itself. There is such a wide choice of plants and flowers available in summer that each detail can be a celebration of a different herb. For example, wrapping flowering rosemary around napkins will encourage your guests to appreciate the plant's delicate purple flower.

For your tablecloth, choose a pale natural fabric such as undyed linen. This will allow the herbs to hold center stage rather than making them compete with a busy pattern. Height is important in any table setting, and one easy way to achieve it is to decorate candlesticks or candelabra. Soak a foam brick in water. (These can be bought from florists and, if kept damp, will maintain the freshness of the the herbs for days.) Slice off two chunks, one for each side of the candlestick, and use floral tape to wrap them together. Rosemary, eucalyptus, lemon balm, parsley, flowering apple mint, and various

Intensify the pleasures of summer dining by combining the delicate scents of freshly cut flowers and herbs with the stronger aromas of herbs used in cooking and the spicy flavors of salad herbs.

Each place setting is adorned with a herbal napkin ring, a finger bowl sprinkled with aromatic herbs, and a miniature pot of herbs that acts as a holder for placecards.

pelargoniums make a good base. You can then introduce more delicate herbs and flowers such as flowering coriander and old-fashioned scented roses. Combining culinary herbs and scent-giving herbs in a table decoration can produce very satisfying results, especially if the culinary herbs have also been used in the preparation of food.

As with the tablecloth, choose plain or understated china, flatware, and glassware that will not upstage the greenery. Arrange the herbs loosely; think about how they grow in the garden and let them ramble across the table. Herbs wilt quickly, so make sure they are in plenty of water. Spray loose herbs with water half an hour before your guests sit down, to keep the table looking fresh.

OPPOSITE PAGE, LEFT **A sprig of rosemary tied loosely around a crisp linen napkin is a pretty alternative to a napkin ring.**

OPPOSITE PAGE, RIGHT **The woody stems of lemon balm are easily woven into lattice-pattern placemats. When a hot plate is placed on a mat, a delicious aroma is released.**

ABOVE **Float leaves of mint and lemon balm in small glass bowls of water so your visitors can rinse their fingers between courses.**

ABOVE RIGHT **Write the names of your guests on copper plant tags and put them in miniature terra cotta plant pots filled with fresh herbs.**

A bowl of freshly torn herbs such as basil, mint, tarragon, cilantro, and flat-leaved parsley is an attractive detail—and guests can help themselves to handfuls to sprinkle on their food.

If you have a conservatory to dine in, or if your dining room is full of natural light, take advantage of this environment to grow herbs in containers (see pages 54–55). Surround the table with pots of delicious-smelling culinary and aromatic herbs. For containers that are intended to be a permanent feature, choose unusual items such as china basins and chimney pots. Trailing herbs in hanging baskets make romantic decorations; suitable varieties include prostrate rosemary, prostrate sage, creeping thymes, catnip, and the colorful nasturtium.

Although they may seem out of place in an office, herbs can do much to enhance your working environment. Particular varieties invigorate and uplift the mind, aiding concentration and inspiration. Keep a pot of fresh herbs on your desk or near your work area, where the leaves and flowers will be lovely to look at and will gently fragrance the air.

Essential oils sprinkled onto a tissue or handkerchief are an alternative to fresh herbs and provide a stronger herbal "hit." Basil is energizing and invigorating, and is used to treat depression. Cilantro and eucalpytus are also uplifting. Geranium is refreshing and relaxing, as is lavender. Lemon balm bursts with zingy fragrance, and thyme is good for combating depression and fatigue.

Even the paper you use can be scented—either buy it ready-scented or add a few drops of essential oil. Stick dried herbs to paper or leave them loose in a folded letter. A sophisticated flower press is not needed. Simply take a perfect flower or leaf and sandwich it between two piles of blotting or watercolor paper. Put this sandwich between the leaves of a large heavy book and pile three or four more heavy books on top of it. Leave for a couple of weeks, until the herbs have dried out.

Ink, too, can be fragranced. Immerse 1 oz. (25 g) of dried aromatic flowers (such as myrtle, lavender flowers, lemon verbena, pelargonium, or rosemary) in water and bring to a boil. Simmer for 30–40 minutes until it has reduced to 4 teaspoons of pungent dark liquid. Strain, let it cool, and add to a bottle of ordinary ink.

ABOVE **As a powerful aid to concentration, place a pitcher of fresh herbs such as basil and mint on a desk or elsewhere in a work space.**

RIGHT **Writing paper can be scented with a few drops of essential oil and decorated with dried pressed herbs. Even the ink you use to write a letter can be fragranced.**

Refreshing and
invigorating herbs
can bring a new
sense of purpose
to your working
space, and revive
some of the almost
forgotten pleasures
of letter writing.

LEFT **Herbs with colorful and
pretty blooms can be dried
and pressed the same way
as any wildflowers before
being incorporated into
eye-catching arrangements.**

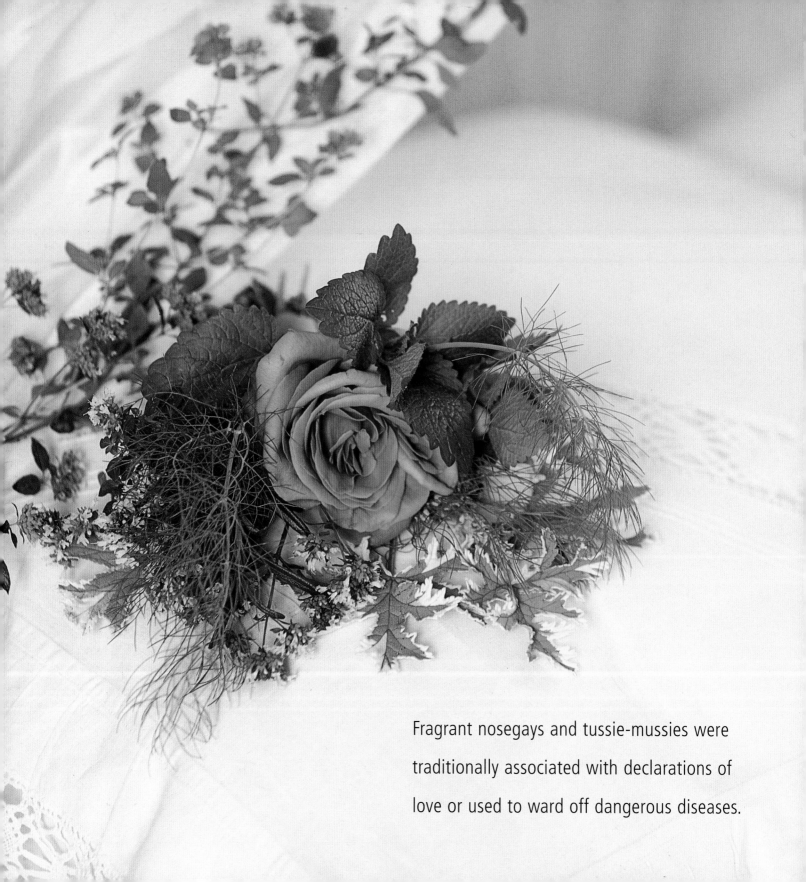

Fragrant nosegays and tussie-mussies were traditionally associated with declarations of love or used to ward off dangerous diseases.

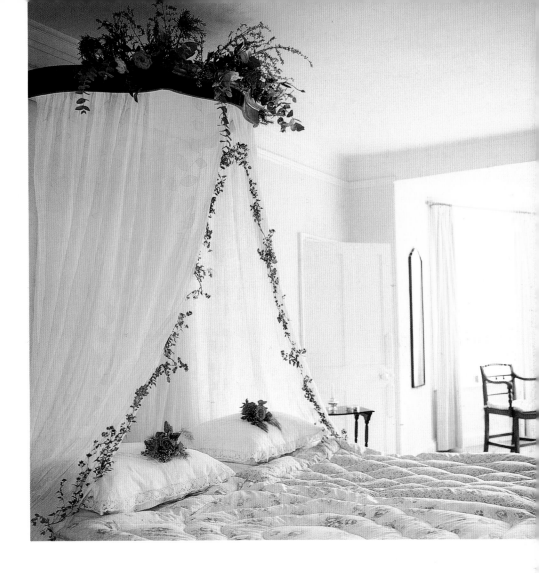

LEFT **This tussie-mussie includes flowering thyme for courage, fennel for strength, lemon balm for sympathy, and geranium for comfort.**

RIGHT **A bridal bed decorated with fresh flowering thyme, rosemary, pelargoniums, eucalyptus, and roses looks romantic and will fill a room with fresh summer smells.**

Nosegays or tussie-mussies—posies made up of aromatic herbs and flowers—were popular from medieval times, not only because of their ability to disguise unlovely smells, but also because they were thought to protect the holder from disease. They were also used for declarations of love, since all the flowers and herbs had special meanings. A lover might send a posy of, for example, mint for virtue, forget-me-nots for true love, golden marjoram for blushes, myrtle for love, rosemary for remembrance, and ivy for fidelity. Guests will be sure to appreciate such a posy placed on a pillow or at the bedside, even if they have no idea of the signficance of the herbs and flowers used.

To fill a bedroom with summer scent in winter, spray bed linen with a fresh linen spray or sprinkle pillows with a diluted essential oil. Chamomile, lavender, lemon balm, and oregano promote sound sleep.

## Garlanded with scent

ABOVE **Catnip's long woody stems are easy to loop into a fresh herbal garland.**

ABOVE RIGHT **Its strength and pliability make dried lavender ideal for bending and weaving into shape.**

To scent a room in winter, when fresh herbs are scarce, you can vaporize an essential herbal oil in a ceramic burner. Add 3 or 4 drops of the oil of your choice to water in the bowl of the burner and use a nightlight to heat it gently from beneath.

Like potpourri, garlands are designed to scent the air and the objects around them, but in a more decorative way. They can be hung on the backs of doors and the corners of beds, or simply placed on a pillow to welcome a guest. Only herbs with tough and pliable stems can be used to make garlands because they must be able to withstand being looped and twisted. For fresh herbal garlands use catnip, lemon balm, lemon verbena, marjoram, mint, and scented pelargoniums. Rosemary, lavender, bay, myrtle, and eucalpytus are rewarding to use either fresh or dried.

THIS PAGE **The scent of lavender has a relaxing effect and promotes sound sleep, so it is a particularly appropriate herb for decorative use in the bedroom.**

An aromatic herbal bath is one of the most pleasurable ways to cleanse your skin and revitalize your whole body. You can add particular herbs to promote relaxation or stimulation.

ABOVE **Put a bar of herbal soap on a bed of fresh mint. An invigorating aroma is released when the leaves are gently crushed.**

ABOVE CENTER **Hang a bunch of fresh herbs from the hot-water faucet before the tub is filled with water. Lemon balm and eucalyptus have a wonderfully revitalizing effect in the morning.**

LEFT AND ABOVE RIGHT **Scatter fresh lavender around the tub and put down a cotton mat to stand on. The scent of crushed lavender fills the bathroom and permeates nearby rooms.**

Some herbs invigorate; others soothe the mind and body, promoting peaceful sleep. For stimulation, choose basil, bay, rosemary, eucalyptus, lemon verbena, mint, sage, and thyme. For relaxation, the preferred herbs are chamomile, lavender, and lemon balm.

To treat minor skin irritations or to soothe dry sensitive skin, use calendula, comfrey, fennel, lady's mantle, parsley, and spearmint. Any of these herbs can be used,

in dried form, in a herbal bath. The herbs should be crushed or ground and put into a gauze bag; hang the bag under a hot faucet before filling the tub.

The water in a herbal bath should be close to body temperature; if it is too hot, the skin perspires and fails to take advantage of the therapeutic qualities. To enjoy the full benefits of the bath, wallow in it for at least 10 minutes.

**Therapeutic preparations** can be made at home from essential oils and herbal infusions.

## lavender spritz

For a classic skin freshener, fill an atomizer bottle with distilled water and add a couple of drops of lavender oil. Shake to blend.

## hand cream

*1 cup (250 ml) rosewater*
*¼ cup (60 ml) glycerin*
*¼ cup (60 ml) cornstarch*
*3 drops chamomile oil*

Blend rosewater, cornstarch, and glycerin. Heat gently in a double boiler to thicken, then cool. Stir in oil. Store in screw-top jar.

## lip balm

*Oil of eucalyptus, lemon, thyme, jasmine, lavender, geranium, juniper, or peppermint*

Add 2 drops of the oil of your choice to 1 tablespoon of warmed cocoa butter. Put in a small jar and let it cool.

## rosewater toner

*⅔ cup (150 ml) rosewater*
*⅔ cup (150 ml) witch hazel*
*6 drops glycerin*

Pour all the ingredients into a bottle and shake well before use.

## vinegar bath

Boil leaves of lemon balm and pennyroyal in cider vinegar. Infuse overnight, then strain. Pour into warm water for a refreshing bath.

## massage oil

*5 drops lavender oil*
*5 drops neroli oil*
*6 drops frankincense*
*¼ cup (60 ml) almond oil*

Add oils to a small stoppered jar and shake to blend. Massage gently into the skin to firm it up and to combat stretch marks.

## foot bath

*Fresh leaves of bay, eucalyptus, lavender, lemon balm, thyme, marjoram, spearmint*

Sprinkle handfuls of herbs into a large bowl. Add 2 teaspoons of salt and enough hot water to cover the feet and ankles. Soak feet for at least 10 minutes while breathing in the delicious aroma.

## antiseptic wash

Among oils with antiseptic action are thyme, lavender, tea tree, and eucalyptus. Add 8 drops of one of these to a small bowl of water and apply to minor wounds.

*Essential oils should not be used undiluted, nor taken internally except on medical advice.*

Essential herbal
oils or fresh herbs
steeped in hot water
can be used to create
a wide variety of
bathroom tonics—or
simply to enhance
the luxury of bathing.

cooking with herbs

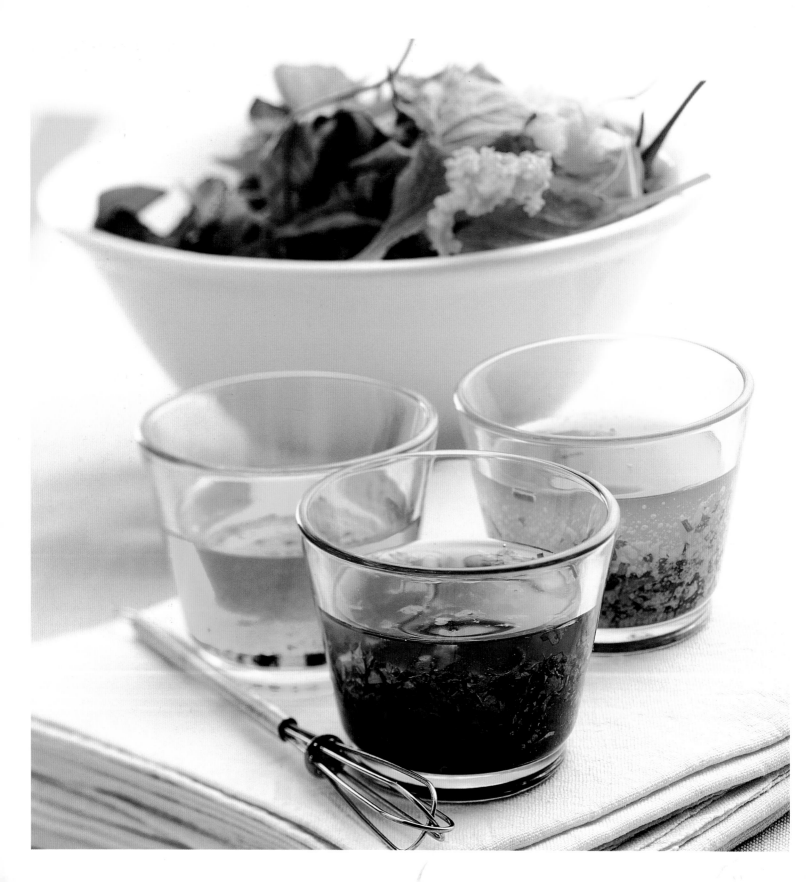

# vinegars, dressings, oils, and butters

Vinegars and dressings take on a slightly exotic flavor when combined with herbs, and there are many herbs that are good for this purpose. Flavored vinegars enhance fruit syrups and salad dressings—or can be used to deglaze a pan in which meat or fish has been fried.

## tarragon vinegar

**2 sprigs of tarragon (or thyme, lavender, or chives)**
**2 cups (500 ml) white wine vinegar**

**Makes 2 cups (500 ml)**

Put the herb in the vinegar and leave in a warm sunny place for 3 or 4 days to let the flavor develop. Use as required.

## tarragon vinegar dressing

**1 tablespoon tarragon vinegar**
**¼ cup hazelnut oil**
**2 tablespoons extra virgin olive oil**
**½ teaspoon sugar**
**salt and freshly ground black pepper**

Make the tarragon vinegar as described above. Then stir all the ingredients and use as required.

## mixed herb dressing

The different combinations of herbs that can be used to make this dressing are virtually endless.

**2 tablespoons chopped mixed herbs: basil, chervil, chives, parsley, and mint**
**½ cup (125 ml) extra virgin olive oil**
**1 tablespoon balsamic vinegar**
**1 tablespoon Dijon mustard**
**1 garlic clove, lightly crushed**
**salt and freshly ground black pepper**

**Makes ⅔ cup (150 ml)**

Beat the chopped herbs into the olive oil. Beat in the vinegar and mustard. Season to taste, then add the garlic.

Use at once or store in the refrigerator for up to 2 days. Return the dressing to room temperature before use.

## cilantro, soy, and sesame dressing

In addition to giving a refreshing zing to hearty vegetable salads, this dressing is delicious trickled over broiled chicken or sautéed and sliced duck breast.

**2 tablespoons chopped cilantro**
**1 tablespoon dark soy sauce**
**1 teaspoon clear honey**
**1 teaspoon wholegrain mustard**
**2 teaspoons rice vinegar**
**1 tablespoon sesame oil**
**⅓ cup peanut oil**

**Makes ½ cup (125 ml)**

Beat all the ingredients together and use as required.

## basil oil

You can enhance the flavor of a tomato salad and add color contrast by tossing the tomatoes gently in basil oil.

*¾ cup (25 g) basil (or parsley)*
*   leaves*
*1¼ cups (300 ml) extra virgin*
*   olive oil*
*a pinch of salt*

*Makes about 1 cup (250 ml)*

Put the basil leaves, oil, and salt in a food processor and blend to make a vivid green paste. Infuse overnight, then strain the oil through a layer of cheesecloth. Use the oil as required or store it in the refrigerator. Return it to room temperature before use.

## thyme, lemon, and chile oil

For a warming supper, toss cooked pasta in a good dash of this oil, then top with sautéed mushrooms and a sprinkling of freshly grated pecorino cheese.

*4 sprigs of thyme*
*4 pieces of lemon zest,*
*   cut into thin strips*
*2 small red chiles, finely sliced*
*2½ cups (600 ml) extra virgin*
*   olive oil*

*Makes about 2½ cups (600 ml)*

Put the thyme, lemon strips, and sliced chiles in a bottle and add the oil. Infuse for 7–10 days, then strain into a clean bottle.

## fragrant Thai oil

This subtly spiced oil is wonderful trickled over steamed fish or added to marinades.

*2 stalks of lemongrass,*
*   halved lengthwise*
*6 kaffir lime leaves or lime zest*
*2 slices galangal or fresh ginger*
*1 tiny red chile*
*2½ cups (600 ml) sunflower oil*

*Makes about 2½ cups (600 ml)*

Lightly crush the herbs and aromatics and put them in a wide-necked bottle. Top up with the sunflower oil.

Leave to infuse for 7–10 days in a cool place before using.

## rosemary, garlic, and pepper oil

To savor the delights of this pungently aromatic oil, use it as a dip for focaccia or ciabatta bread. An alternative is to trickle it over a freshly baked pizza (see page 98).

*4 sprigs of rosemary*
*2 garlic cloves, sliced*
*1 tablespoon black peppercorns,*
*   lightly crushed*
*2½ cups (600 ml) extra virgin*
*   olive oil*

*Makes about 2½ cups (600 ml)*

Put the rosemary, sliced garlic, and peppercorns into a small saucepan with the olive oil. Heat gently until just boiling and simmer for 1 minute. Let cool, then infuse overnight.

The following day, strain the infused oil into a clean bottle and add a sprig of rosemary and a few whole black peppercorns for decoration.

Combining herbs and oils is a terrific way both to preserve the herbs and to jazz up the oils.

Flavored oils shouldn't be confined to salads. Use in marinades, trickle over broiled or grilled

meat or fish—or pour into a dish and serve as a dip with a selection of freshly baked breads.

Herb butters add a lovely finishing touch to cooked fish or chicken and are easy to make. Simply beat your favorite herb into some softened butter, perhaps adding a little pepper or lemon juice. Cover with plastic wrap and chill until required.

## fennel and lemon butter

The flavor of fennel goes very well with fish. For a particularly satisfying result, melt 1 tablespoon of the butter into a piece of fried salmon fillet.

*1 stick (100 g) lightly salted butter,*
*  softened*
*2 tablespoons chopped fennel fronds*
*grated zest of half a lemon*
*a little freshly ground black pepper*

*Makes about ½ cup (100 g)*

Put the butter, fennel, lemon zest, and pepper in a bowl and beat them until the butter is evenly speckled green. Pat it into a roll, cover with plastic wrap, and chill.

## cilantro and scallion butter

The pungency of cilantro and the sweetness of scallion combine to make a butter that can give a new meaning to mashed potatoes.

*1 stick (100 g) lightly salted butter,*
*  softened*
*2 tablespoons chopped cilantro*
*1 scallion, finely chopped*

*Makes about ½ cup (100 g)*

Follow the method for making fennel and lemon butter, but replace the fronds of fennel with the cilantro and scallion. Chill until required. Beat into hot mashed potatoes.

## pepper and chive butter

Roasted cod fillets taste even better when topped with this mildly onion-flavored butter.

*1 stick (100 g) lightly salted butter,*
*  softened*
*2 tablespoons chopped chives*
*1 tablespoon mixed peppercorns,*
*  lightly crushed*

*Makes about ½ cup (100 g)*

Follow the method for making fennel and lemon butter, but replace the fronds of fennel with the chives and peppercorns. Chill until required. Serve with roasted fillets of cod or other white fish.

# snacks and appetizers

## ricotta baked with fresh herbs and chile

This is an easy way to cook ricotta that makes an ideal light lunch. Small rounds of ricotta are available from most Italian gourmet stores—or use wedges cut from a larger cheese.

1 lb. (500 g) ricotta cheese
2 garlic cloves, sliced
1 red chile, seeded and sliced
½ teaspoon lightly crushed coriander seeds
¼ cup extra virgin olive oil
4 fresh bay leaves, lightly crushed
1 tablespoon freshly grated Parmesan cheese,
  plus extra to serve
salt and freshly ground black pepper
basil oil (page 90) or salsa verde (page 96)
  and toasted bread, to serve

Serves 4–6

Put the ricotta in a foil-lined baking dish. Put the garlic, chile, coriander seeds, and oil in a bowl and stir. Trickle the oil mixture over the cheese and tuck the bay leaves underneath.

Sprinkle Parmesan, salt and pepper over the ricotta and bake in a preheated oven at 375°F (190°C) for 20 minutes, basting halfway through the cooking time.

Serve the ricotta spread onto toasted bread sprinkled with basil oil or salsa verde. Serve topped with a little grated Parmesan.

Herb-based sauces or spreads can be served as dips for crudités or spooned onto broiled or grilled fish or poultry. Zhatar is a Middle Eastern street snack traditionally sold rolled up in a cone of paper with hard-cooked eggs.

## salsa verde

*¾ cup (25 g) parsley leaves*
*⅓ cup (15 g) mixed herbs, such as basil, chives, cilantro, and mint*
*1 garlic clove, chopped*
*6 green olives, pitted*
*1 tablespoon capers, rinsed and drained*
*2 anchovy fillets, rinsed and chopped*
*1 teaspoon Dijon mustard*
*2 teaspoons lemon juice*
*½ cup (125 ml) extra virgin olive oil*
*salt and freshly ground black pepper*
*vegetables and bread, to serve*

*Serves 6*

Put all the ingredients, except the oil, in a food mixer and blend to form a smooth paste. Gradually blend in the oil to form a sauce, then add salt and pepper to taste.

Serve as a dip with a selection of raw or cooked vegetables and fresh bread.

## zhatar

*⅓ cup (15 g) thyme leaves*
*1½ tablespoons sesame seeds, toasted*
*¼ teaspoon salt*

*Serves 4*

Put the ingredients in a mixer and work to a fine powder. Serve with hard-cooked eggs.

## zhug

*¾ cup (25 g) cilantro leaves*
*2–4 garlic cloves*
*1 teaspoon caraway seeds*
*1 teaspoon cumin seeds*
*seeds from 3 cardamom pods*
*1 large red chile, seeded and diced*
*2 tablespoons extra virgin olive oil*
*salt and freshly ground black pepper*

*Serves 4*

Put all the ingredients in a food processor and blend until smooth. Add salt and pepper to taste and serve with grilled pita or lavash bread.

# little pizzas with herb oil

This is a variation on hot garlic bread, in which small, thin pizza crusts are doused in rosemary, garlic, and pepper oil.

*1 cup (150 g) white bread flour*
*1 teaspoon quick-rising active dry yeast*
*1 teaspoon salt*
*1 tablespoon extra virgin olive oil (or a flavored oil)*

*herb topping*
*2 large garlic cloves, sliced*
*leaves from 4 sprigs of rosemary*
*rosemary, garlic, and pepper oil (page 90)*

*Makes 4 small or 2 large pizzas*

Sift the flour into the bowl of a food mixer and stir in the yeast and salt. With the dough hook turning, slowly pour in the oil and about ½ cup (125 ml) water heated to 120°F (48°C), to form a slightly sticky dough.

Knead for 10 minutes. Shape the dough into a ball. Put it in a greased bowl, cover with plastic wrap, and let rise for about 1 hour until the ball has doubled in size. Heat the oven to 450°F (230°C) and put a pizza stone or cookie sheet on the top shelf to heat.

Punch down the dough and divide it into 2 or 4 pieces. Put one piece on a floured surface and roll it out to form a thin, round crust. Mix the rosemary leaves and garlic with 6–8 tablespoons rosemary, garlic, and pepper oil and sprinkle a little of the mixture over the pizza crust.

Transfer the crust to the heated pizza stone or cookie sheet and bake for 10–12 minutes until puffed and golden. Sprinkle with a little extra rosemary, garlic, and pepper oil. Continue to roll out and cook the pizzas one at a time, eating them as they come out of the oven.

# Vietnamese herb and shrimp rolls

Rice noodles, shrimp, and fragrant herbs are rolled up in rice paper wrappers and served with *nuóc cham*— a traditional Vietnamese dipping sauce.

Start by making the *nuóc cham*. Put the fish sauce, sugar, chile, and lime juice in a bowl. Add 2 tablespoons water and let infuse for 1 hour.

Cook the noodles in a large saucepan of lightly salted, boiling water for 3 minutes. Drain and refresh them in cold water. Drain again. Mix the noodles with 1 tablespoon of the dipping sauce.

To rehydrate the rice paper wrappers, dip them one by one into a bowl of cold water for a few seconds until they are soft.

Lay each wrapper flat and top with a small handful of cooked noodles, 2 or 3 shrimp, a few pea shoots or bean sprouts, and a few herb leaves.

Fold over the ends of the wrappers and roll up to enclose the filling. Serve with the dipping sauce.

**nuóc cham**
**3 tablespoons fish sauce**
**2 tablespoons sugar**
**1 large red chile, seeded and finely chopped**
*juice of ½ lime*

**1 bundle (2 oz./60 g) of beanthread or vermicelli rice noodles**
**12 small rice paper wrappers (available from Chinese supermarkets)**
**24–36 large cooked shrimp, shelled**
**1 cup (50 g) pea shoots or bean sprouts**
**12 Thai basil leaves (optional)**
**12 mint leaves**
**12 cilantro leaves**

*Serves 6*

# entrées

## sea bass with fragrant Thai oil

For this dish you need either 2 woks or 2 large bamboo steamers. The easiest way to cook the fish is to lay them on large pieces of foil and put these on the racks of the woks or in the bottom of the steamers, so all the delicious juices settle in the foil.

Wash and dry the sea bass inside and out, and slash each side diagonally several times with a sharp knife. Put 2 fish on each of 2 large sheets of foil.

Mix the ginger, onion, and garlic in a bowl. Put some of the mixture into each cavity and add a few slices of lime and a couple of cilantro sprigs. Sprinkle the rest over the fish.

Mix the tamari, mirin, and 2 tablespoons of the Thai oil together in a pitcher or bowl, then trickle the mixture over the fish. Put each foil package on racks set in 2 separate woks or into the bottom of 2 steamers. Cover tightly with lids and steam for 12 minutes. Remove from the heat, but leave undisturbed for 5 minutes longer.

Sprinkle each fish with chopped cilantro and serve it with the juices, steamed rice, and steamed Chinese greens.

*4 sea bass, 1 lb. (500 g) each, drawn and scaled*
*2 inches (5 cm) fresh ginger, peeled and sliced*
*4 scallions, finely chopped*
*2 garlic cloves, sliced*
*1 lime, sliced*
*4 large sprigs of cilantro*
*¼ cup tamari (Japanese soy sauce)*
*2 tablespoons mirin (sweetened Japanese rice wine)*
*⅓ cup fragrant Thai oil (see page 90)*
*chopped cilantro leaves, steamed rice, and Chinese greens, to serve*

*Serves 4*

# red mullet saltimbocca with orange and sage

The Italian saltimbocca of veal scallop topped by prosciutto ham and sage inspired this dish. Red mullet is a rich fish, able to take the strong flavors of both ham and herb. The sweet/sharp sauce of orange and capers is a perfect foil. If red mullet is not available, substitute striped bass.

*2 oranges*
*8 large red mullet fillets, scaled*
*freshly ground black pepper*
*8 slices prosciutto*
*16 large sage leaves*
*3 tablespoons extra virgin olive oil*
*2 tablespoons (25 g) lightly salted butter*
*2 tablespoons capers, rinsed and drained*
*⅓ cup (75 ml) white wine*

*Serves 4*

Peel and segment one of the oranges, reserving the juices in a bowl. Squeeze the juice of the other orange into the bowl.

Wash and dry the fish fillets and season them with pepper. Lay the prosciutto slices flat and top each with a fillet and a sage leaf. Trickle a little oil over the top. Starting from one narrow end, carefully roll up each piece of ham, enclosing the fillet, and secure it with a toothpick.

Heat the remaining oil and the butter together in a skillet with a heatproof handle. Add the rolls of fish and quickly brown them on all sides. Add the capers, wine, orange juice, and remaining sage leaves. Cover with a layer of foil and bake in a preheated oven at 400°F (200°C) for 8 minutes. Remove from the oven, transfer the rolls to a warm plate, and let rest for 5 minutes.

Meanwhile, add the orange segments to the skillet and heat through on top of the stove. Serve the saltimbocca with the sauce, a green salad, and some bread to mop up the delicious juices.

# chile beef with avocado and cilantro salsa

The chile-marinated steaks can be broiled or cooked on an outdoor grill. The heat of the chile sauce is tempered by the coolness of the avocado and the sour cream. For a great picnic sandwich, let the steaks cool, then slice them and stuff each into a pita pocket with a spoonful of the salsa and another of sour cream.

*4 beef filet mignons, about 8 oz. (250 g) each*
*2 tablespoons hot chile sauce or harissa paste*
*2 tablespoons olive oil*
*¼ cup (60 ml) sour cream*
*sprigs of cilantro, to serve*

*avocado and cilantro salsa*
*1 large ripe Hass avocado*
*2 ripe tomatoes, peeled, seeded, and diced*
*freshly squeezed juice of ½ to 1 lime*
*1 garlic clove, crushed*
*1 small red chile, seeded and diced*
*2 tablespoons chopped cilantro*
*1 tablespoon extra virgin olive oil*
*salt and freshly ground black pepper*

*Serves 4*

Put the steaks in a shallow dish and rub them all over with the chile sauce and oil. Marinate at room temperature for 1–4 hours.

Just before cooking the steaks, cut the avocado in half and remove the pit. Using a teaspoon, scoop the flesh into a bowl. Stir in the tomato, lime juice, garlic, chile, cilantro, and oil. Season with salt and pepper.

Heat a stove-top grill pan for 3–4 minutes until it is very hot. Add the steaks and cook for 2 minutes each side. Set aside to rest for 5 minutes.

Serve the steaks topped with the avocado and cilantro salsa, the sour cream, and sprigs of cilantro.

*1 chicken, about 3½ lb. (1.75 kg)*
*¾ cup (25 g) fresh curry leaves or*
  *⅓ cup (15 g) dried*
*1 stick (100 g) lightly salted butter*
*1 lemon, halved*
*1 whole head of garlic,*
  *cloves separated*
*salt and freshly ground*
  *black pepper*

*Serves 4*

# butter-roasted chicken
# with curry leaves

In some neighborhoods, the leaves of the curry plant
are sold fresh or dried at Asian food stores. If they are
not available, substitute sprigs of tarragon.

Wash the chicken and pat dry with paper towels. Season the cavity
with salt and pepper and add a couple of sprigs of curry leaves. Cut
several slashes in the flesh of each thigh. Finely chop (or tear) most of
the remaining curry leaves. Put them in a bowl and beat in the butter
with a wooden spoon.

Release the skin of the chicken from the flesh by inserting 4 of your
fingers under the skin at the neck end. Lift the skin away from the
breast meat and push half the butter mixture under it, smoothing
until it is flat. Rub the remaining butter all over the outside of the
skin, pushing it down into the slashes. Squeeze the juice of ½ lemon
over the chicken and put the other half into the cavity.

Arrange the garlic cloves and remaining curry leaves in a roasting pan.
Put the chicken on top and roast in a preheated oven at 400°F (200°C)
for about 1 hour 5 minutes. Pierce the thickest part of the thigh with
a skewer, penetrating as far as the joint: if the juices run clear, the
chicken is cooked through. Let it rest for 5 minutes before carving.

# spring herb risotto

The flavors of the herbs blend with the creaminess of the rice and cheese in this light, fragrant risotto. It is particularly good topped with a seared fillet of salmon or sautéed cod.

*1 cup (50 g) shredded baby spinach leaves*
*1½ cups (50 g) chopped mixed herbs, such*
*as chervil, chives, mint, parsley, and*
*tarragon*
*¼ cup extra virgin olive oil*
*1 onion, finely chopped*
*2 garlic cloves, crushed*
*2 small leeks, well washed,*
*    trimmed, and sliced*
*1½ cups (300 g) arborio rice*
*⅔ cup (150 ml) dry white wine*
*¼ cup Mascarpone cheese*
*½ cup (50 g) freshly grated Parmesan*
*    cheese, plus extra to serve*
*salt and freshly ground black pepper*

*Serves 4*

Put 5 cups (1.25 litres) water in a large saucepan and heat to a rolling boil. Add the spinach and herbs, return to a boil, and immediately strain, reserving the liquid. Refresh the spinach and herbs under cold water. Pat dry with paper towels and set aside.

Heat the oil in a deep fryer. Add the onion, garlic, and leek and fry slowly for 10 minutes. Add the rice and stir the mixture over the heat for 1 minute until all the grains are glossy. Pour in the wine and boil until almost totally evaporated.

In a separate saucepan, heat the reserved herb water until just simmering. Add the water to the rice, 1 ladle at a time, and simmer, stirring, until absorbed, before adding more. Repeat until all the water has been used and the rice is tender but still firm.

Stir in spinach, herbs, and Mascarpone and Parmesan cheeses. Cover and let stand for 5 minutes. Season with salt and pepper. Serve with extra Parmesan.

# accompaniments

## mixed leaf and herb salad with pine nut dressing

The pine nuts add a rich, creamy flavor and texture to this salad dressing, which perfectly complements the aromatic herbs and leaves. Mix a good selection of fresh herbs—basil, chervil, chives, dill, mint, and parsley, for example—with salad leaves such as arugula, romaine, frisée, ruby chard, dandelion greens, and mizuna.

*6 cups (500 g) mixed leaves and 2½ cups (100 g) mixed herbs*

*pine nut dressing*
*2 tablespoons pine nuts*
*¼ cup extra virgin olive oil*
*2 teaspoons sherry vinegar*
*salt and freshly ground pepper*

*Serves 4*

Put the salad leaves and herbs in a very large bowl.

To make the dressing, heat 2 tablespoons of the oil in a skillet. Add the pine nuts and sauté for 3–4 minutes until evenly golden. Let cool.

Using a mortar and pestle, smash the nuts until they are mushy. Stir in the remaining oil. Add the vinegar, and season to taste. Pour the dressing over the salad and toss well until all the leaves are coated. Serve at once.

## charred leek salad with tarragon vinegar dressing

In this "smoky" salad the charred peppers and leeks are well set off by the sharpness of the tarragon-infused vinegar dressing, which must be made in advance.

*2 small red bell peppers*
*12 oz. (350 g) baby leeks, well washed and trimmed*
*olive oil*
*1 cup (125 g) French beans, trimmed*
*3 cups (125 g) baby spinach leaves*
*½ cup (50 g) pitted black olives*
*1 quantity tarragon vinegar dressing (see page 89)*
*salt and freshly ground pepper*
*Parmesan shavings, to serve*

*Serves 4*

Heat a large stove-top grill pan for 3 minutes. Add the whole peppers and cook for 10–15 minutes, turning occasionally, until charred all over. Transfer to a bowl, cover with a clean dry cloth, and let cool.

Toss the leeks in a little oil. Add to the grill pan and cook over low heat for 10–12 minutes until evenly charred. Let cool and cut in half crosswise. At the same time, blanch the beans in a large saucepan of lightly salted, boiling water for 3–4 minutes. Drain, refresh under cold water, and pat dry.

Slip the skins off the peppers, cut them in half, and remove all the seeds. Cut the flesh into strips and toss the strips with the charred leeks and the beans. Arrange on a large plate. Add the spinach leaves and olives to the salad. Sprinkle with plenty of the salad dressing. Add the Parmesan shavings and serve at once.

## smashed celery root with horseradish

The grated horseradish makes this deliciously rich "smash" a good partner for roast beef—or substitute chopped mint for the parsley and serve with broiled lamb chops.

*¼ cup extra virgin olive oil, plus extra to mash*
*2 garlic cloves, crushed*
*6 scallions, trimmed and chopped*
*3¼ cups (500 g) peeled and finely diced celery root*
*3¼ cups (500 g) peeled and finely diced potatoes*
*2 inch piece of horseradish, peeled and finely grated*
*  (or 3 tablespoons ready-grated)*
*1¼ cups (300 ml) vegetable stock*
*2 tablespoons chopped flat-leaved parsley*
*salt and freshly ground black pepper*

*Serves 4*

Heat the oil in a saucepan. Add the garlic and onion and sauté slowly for 5 minutes. Remove with a draining spoon and set aside. Add the celery root, potatoes, and horseradish to the pan and sauté for 5 minutes.

Pour the stock into the saucepan and bring to a boil. Cover and simmer for 25–30 minutes until the vegetables are tender. Remove the lid and boil until the liquid is reduced to the point where almost nothing remains and the mixture is sticky.

Stir in the reserved garlic and onion. Add the parsley, salt, and pepper and mash coarsely with a fork, beating in more olive oil to taste.

## slow-roasted tomato salad with opal basil

This pretty salad can be served either as an accompaniment, a light lunch, or an appetizer. When opal basil leaves are not available, ordinary green basil can be used instead.

*6 ripe tomatoes, halved*
*1 tablespoon olive oil*
*12 oz. mozzarella cheese (preferably buffalo mozzarella)*
*a few sprigs opal basil*
*1 quantity basil oil (see page 90)*
*balsamic vinegar*
*baby salad leaves such as mizuna*
*salt and freshly ground black pepper*

*Serves 4*

Put the halved tomatoes in a small roasting pan in a single layer. Sprinkle with the olive oil and season liberally with salt and pepper. Roast in a heated oven at 300°F (150°C) for 3 hours until shrunken and glossy. Let cool.

Just before serving, tear the mozzarella into small pieces and arrange on a large plate. Add the tomato halves, then sprinkle the opal basil leaves over the tomatoes and cheese. Trickle a generous amount of the basil oil and a little vinegar over the salad. Season to taste with salt and pepper, and serve the salad topped with salad leaves.

# sweet things

## apricots poached in tarragon syrup

A delicately flavored tarragon and vanilla syrup perfumes the fresh apricots while they cook and then cool. The poached fruits can be enjoyed at their best when served with homemade vanilla ice cream or thick, plain yogurt.

*⅔ cup (125 g) sugar*
*2 pieces lemon zest, cut into thin strips*
*1 vanilla bean, split lengthwise*
*6 large sprigs of tarragon, lightly crushed*
*12 apricots, halved and pitted*
*1 tablespoon tarragon vinegar (see page 89)*
*   or lemon juice*
*vanilla ice cream or thick, plain yogurt, to serve*

*Serves 6*

Put the sugar and 1¼ cups (300 ml) water in a wide saucepan and heat slowly to dissolve the sugar. Add the strips of lemon zest, the vanilla bean, and the tarragon sprigs. Bring to a boil.

Add the apricots and simmer slowly for about 5 minutes until soft. Remove the pan from the heat. Stir in the tarragon vinegar or lemon juice and let cool.

Serve with ice cream or yogurt.

# strawberry, melon, and basil salad

This fragrant concoction is best served slightly chilled. The pairing of basil and strawberries is surprisingly good, but other herbs such as fresh mint, lemon verbena, and lemon balm work equally well.

*1 cantaloupe melon, halved, seeded, sliced, and peeled*
*1 basket (250 g) strawberries, hulled and halved*
*¾ cup (180 ml) Muscat de Beaumes de Venise or other sweet wine*
*a few basil leaves*

**Serves 4**

Put the slices of melon in a large bowl with the strawberries. Pour the wine over the fruit and chill for 30 minutes. Top with the basil leaves and serve.

# lemon and rosemary posset with raspberries

The posset in this recipe is a chilled creamy pudding, although originally, in the Middle Ages, a posset was a hot drink. Rosemary goes well with lemon and is excellent in creamy puddings, such as this. The posset should be prepared in advance and chilled overnight in individual dishes.

*1½ cups (600 ml) double cream*
*4 large sprigs of rosemary, washed and bruised*
*½ cup (100 g) sugar*
*½ cup freshly squeezed lemon juice*
*1 cup (125 g) raspberries*
*1 tablespoon framboise liqueur or crème de cassis*

**Serves 6**

Put the cream and rosemary sprigs in a saucepan and heat slowly to boiling point. Remove from the heat and leave to infuse for 20 minutes. Discard the rosemary.

Add the sugar to the cream and return to a boil. Simmer for 3 minutes. Stir in the lemon juice, then immediately pour the mixture into 6 small dishes. Chill overnight.

Marinate the raspberries in framboise or crème de cassis for 30 minutes. Spoon the fruit onto the possets and serve.

# mint chocolate chip ice cream

Heating mint with milk and cream gives this ice cream a wonderfully fresh flavor, which is a million miles away from the synthetically flavored, bright green, ready-made version.

*2 cups (500 ml) whole milk*
*1¼ cups (300 ml) heavy cream*
*4 large sprigs of mint*
*5 egg yolks*
*½ cup plus 2 tablespoons (125 g) superfine sugar*
*3 squares (75 g) semisweet chocolate, cut into small dice*

**Serves 8**

Put the milk, cream, and mint sprigs in a saucepan and heat slowly to boiling point. Remove from the heat and leave to infuse for 20 minutes. Return to boiling point.

Meanwhile, beat the egg yolks and sugar in a bowl. Stir in the hot milk mixture, and return it to the pan. Stir over low heat until the custard is thick enough to coat the back of a wooden spoon. Do not let the mixture boil or it will curdle. Strain into a clean bowl and leave until cold.

Freeze in an ice cream maker according to manufacturer's directions—or freeze in a plastic container, beating at hourly intervals until creamy and frozen. Add the chocolate chips just before the mixture freezes. Serve immediately or freeze until required.

# herbal coolers

## long island tea with lemon verbena

**4 tea bags (India tea is best)**
**a bunch lemon of verbena**
**2 limes, sliced**
**ice cubes**
**lemonade**

**Serves 4**

Place the tea bags in a pitcher and add 4 cups (1 litre) cold water. Chill for 1 hour, then discard the tea bags.

Put the lemon verbena, slices of lime, and plenty of ice cubes in a large clean pitcher. Add the tea and top up with lemonade. Serve cold.

## apple and lemongrass cordial

**4 cups (1 litre) organic apple**
**juice (unsweetened)**
**1¼ cups (250 g) sugar**
**4 large stalks of lemongrass,**
**halved lengthwise**
**lemon wedges, ice cubes, mineral water,**
**and lemongrass stalks, to serve**

**Makes about 3 cups (750 ml)**

Put the apple juice and sugar in a saucepan and heat until the sugar dissolves. Add the lemongrass and simmer for 10 minutes. Let cool, then strain into a clean bottle.

To dilute, pour a little syrup into tall glasses. Add ice cubes and lemon, and top up with still or sparkling mineral water. Add a stalk of lemongrass to each glass and stir well.

## melon and mint frappé

**2 large ripe melons**
**½ cup (15 g) mint leaves**
**freshly squeezed juice of 2 limes**
**a little honey (optional)**
**ice cubes, to serve**

**Serves 4**

Halve, seed, slice, and peel the melon and put the flesh in a blender. Add the mint leaves, lime juice, and honey if using it, and blend until smooth. Serve with ice cubes.

# A–Z of herbs

## A selection of herbs that flavor food or provide garden ornament.

*(Heights given are the maximum heights to which plants can grow in optimum conditions. For key to zones, see page 125.)*

### *Agastache foeniculum*   Z: 6–9
### Anise hyssop

Aromatic, hardy, but short-lived perennial that grows to 2 ft (60 cm) when in flower. Heart-shaped leaves with scalloped edges. Purple or whitish flower spikes in summer. Sow seed in pots in heated propagator in spring. Grows in full sun in average soil, but does best in moist loam. Dried flower spikes and leaves can be added to potpourri.

### *Allium fistulosum*   Z: 4–9
### Welsh onion

Hardy evergreen perennial, also known as scallion or spring onion. Flowers from second year, and reaches 2–3 ft (60–90 cm). Overwinters in coldest conditions. Sow in fertile soil in sun in spring, or divide clumps. Harvest whole onions, or chop leaves as you would chives.

### *Allium sativum*   Z: 4–9
### Garlic

Hardy perennial grown as an annual. Reaches 16–24 in (40–60 cm). Narrow leaves similar to those of leeks. Plant in fall in full sun; harvest as soon as leaves die down. Bulbs are delicious roasted; also used in marinades and salad dressings and to flavor meat. Wild garlic (*A. ursinum*) needs moist woodland conditions; leaves are added to salads and soups.

### *Allium schoenoprasum*   Z: 3–9
### Chives

Hardy perennial with fine green foliage and mauve or white pompom flowers. Depending on species or variety, grows to 12–16 in (30–40 cm) with a spread of 4–8 in (10–20 cm). Grow in full sun in moisture-retentive soil; divide congested clumps in spring or fall. Flowers and leaves are used in salads, egg dishes, and soups. Add to hot dishes at the last moment to prevent loss of flavor.

### *Allium tuberosum*   Z: 3–9
### Chinese chives, garlic chives

Hardy perennial that grows to 16 in (40 cm). Leaves are as long as ordinary chives, but flattened, and have a strong garlic aroma. Sow seed outside in late spring; divide clumps in spring. Good in salads and cooked dishes.

### *Aloe barbadensis*   tropical
### Aloe vera

Succulent half-hardy perennial with fleshy spike-edged leaves. Can grow to 2 ft (60 cm) in a large pot, but is usually much smaller. Sow seed in pots in propagator at 70°F (21°C); germination is erratic—do not lose hope if nothing happens in the first year. Propagate from offshoots in summer. Use loam-based potting soil with added sand. Water sparingly and repot in spring. Plants can be grown outside in summer but must be overwintered in a frost-free place, at a minimum of 40°F (5°C). The gel from its leaf soothes minor burns and cuts; also used in cosmetic preparations.

### *Aloysia triphylla*   Z: 9
### syn. *Lippia citriodora*
### Lemon verbena

Half-hardy deciduous perennial. Grows to 10 ft (3 m) with a spread of 8 ft (2.5 m). Pale-green and lemon-scented lance-shaped leaves; terminal panicles of lilac-tinged white flowers. Likes full sun and free-draining light soil. If grown outside against a sunny wall, needs frost protection. A good deep mulch will keep plant safe in milder climates; in colder areas pot it up and overwinter in frost-free greenhouse. Grow from seed or softwood cuttings in spring. Take cuttings from ripened wood in late summer. A relaxing tisane can be made from the leaves; also used to scent vinegars; dried, it is added to potpourri or herb pillows.

### *Anethum graveolens*   annual
### Dill

Annual varying in height from 2 ft (60 cm) to 5 ft (150 cm). Some varieties are suited to leaf or seed production. Dill needs well-drained, sandy soil and full sun. Sow seed in rows as soon as soil warms up in spring. Thin to about 8 in (20 cm) apart to make sturdy plants. Water in the morning; plants will run to seed if kept too dry. Sow in succession for a good kitchen supply.

### *Angelica archangelica*   Z: 4–9
### Angelica

Biennial or short-lived perennial that dies after flowering. Grows up to 8 ft (2.5 m), but usually 3–5 ft (1–1.5 m). A good ornamental plant in an herb bed in part-shade. Self-seeds copiously. Cooking angelica with rhubarb reduces the need for added sugar; stems can be candied. Should be used medicinally only on medical advice and never by diabetes sufferers.

### *Anthriscus cerefolium*   Z: 3–8
### Chervil

Hardy annual that reaches 1–2 ft (30–60 cm) in flower. Sow seed in light soil. Part shade is best for production of abundant leaves. In a hot dry climate it goes to seed prematurely. A component of the traditional *fines herbes* bundle.

### *Armoracia rusticana*   Z: 3–10
### Horseradish

Hardy perennial that grows to 1–2 ft (60–90 cm). *A. r.* 'Variegata' has prettily marked leaves in cream and green and makes a fine centerpiece in a herb garden (though the flavor is not as good or strong for culinary use as that of the non-variegated type).

*Cichorium intybus* Chicory

*Coriandrum sativum* Cilantro

*Helichrysum italicum* Curry plant

### *Artemisia dracunculus*  Z: 4–7
### Tarragon

French tarragon grows to 3 ft (90 cm); Russian tarragon, *A. dracunculoides*, is slightly taller, reaching 4 ft (1.2 m). Both have a spread of 18 in (45 cm). Grow in a dry sunny site with winter protection. Propagate French tarragon from root cuttings; it is not as hardy as the Russian variety and has no viable seed. Tarragon is good with chicken and fish; French tarragon has much the better flavor.

### *Atriplex hortensis*  annual
### Orach

Annual grown as a culinary and an ornamental herb that reaches 4 ft (1.5 m) or more, with a spread of 12 in (30 cm); can grow taller, depending on the quality of the soil. Seed heads are used in cut-flower arrangements in some countries. Use tender young leaves in cooking: a popular spinach substitute in Europe.

### *Barbarea verna*  Z: 4–8
### Upland cress

Hardy biennial that grows to 8–28 in (20–70 cm) with a spread of about 8 in (20 cm). Sow in rich moist soil, in summer for winter use and in spring for summer use. Prefers sun, but will grow in all but deepest shade. Peppery flavor of leaves makes them a good watercress substitute in salads; use before plant flowers.

### *Borago officinalis*  annual
### Borage

Hardy annual that grows to about 24 in (60 cm); sometimes plants overwinter and grow into a second season. Bristly branches, and leaves with a strong cucumberlike smell; blue or white starlike flowers. Sow seed in spring. Grow in light soil in a sunny position. Edible flowers can be crystallized for decorative use or added fresh to fruit cups. Borage may cause contact dermatitis.

### *Buxus sempervirens*  Z: 5–8
### Boxwood

Hardy to half-hardy evergreen used extensively as an edging plant in herb gardens. Grows from 3 ft (1 m) to 15 ft (5 m), and taller in old unclipped specimens. Leaves are neatly egg-shaped to elliptical, often glossy dark to mid-green, and some cultivars are variegated. Boxwood grows in sun or shade; prefers alkaline soil but, as long as the ground is not waterlogged, is not too fussy. If a hedge is planted, prepare the soil well with compost and well-rotted manure. Take cuttings in spring or summer. Boxwood has no culinary use; all parts are poisonous. It has traditional medical uses.

### *Calendula officinalis*  annual
### Calendula

Hardy annual, but some plants will overwinter successfully. Grows to 24 in (60 cm). Daisylike flowers, single or double, vary in color from pale cream to deep orange. Whole plant is aromatic. Calendula grows in most soils in full sun. Sow seed in spring or fall. Self-sown seedlings are capable of overwintering in sheltered outside positions, but don't rely on this. Deadhead plants regularly to extend flowering season. Culinary and medicinal plant; also used in cosmetic preparations. Dried petals look good in potpourris.

### *Chamaemelum nobile*  Z: 4–8
### Chamomile

Height varies from 2.5 in (6 cm) to 24 in (60 cm) depending on species or cultivar. Non-flowering 'Treneague'—the chamomile commonly used for chamomile lawns—is increased by division and the taking of cuttings, as is the double-flowered chamomile. For others, sow seed in pots or straight into the ground; use bottom heat for pots in spring and sow in ground when it has warmed up. Grow in free-draining soil in full sun. Main uses are cosmetic and medicinal.

### *Chenopodium bonus-henricus*
### Good King Henry  Z: 3–10

Hardy perennial that can reach 24 in (60 cm) with a spread of 18 in (45 cm). Sow seed in fertile soil in spring in a sunny position. Thin out to 10 in (25 cm) apart. Leaves used as a spinach substitute. Seeds are mildly laxative; do not use if you suffer from kidney problems or rheumatism.

### *Cichorium intybus*  Z: 3–10
### Chicory

Hardy perennial reaching a height in flower of 3 ft (1 m). Leaves are long, blunt, and spear-shaped, with coarsely toothed edges. Blue flowers from summer to fall. Sow seed in spring in open sunny situation; prefers alkaline soil but will grow almost anywhere. Leaves are added to salads.

### *Coriandrum sativum*  annual
### Cilantro, coriander

Tender annual growing to 24–28 in (60–70 cm) with a spread of about 12 in (30 cm). *C.s.* 'Cilantro' is best for leaf production and *C.s.* 'Morocco' for seed. Sow seed in spring in a light well-drained soil when threat of frost has passed and soil has warmed up. Thin seedlings as they grow and keep watered for leaf production, but do not overwater. Seeds and leaves are used in cooking and medicinally.

### Cryptotaenia japonica    Z: 4–9
**mitsuba, Japanese parsley**

Hardy perennial that grows to 12 in (30 cm) before flowering and 2–3 ft (60–90 cm) in flower. Leaf is like celery; small umbels of white flowers. Likes moist conditions in part shade. Grows in sun or in the shade of larger plants in moisture-retentive soil. Leaves and stems used in cooking.

### Curcuma longa    tropical
**Turmeric**

Perennial tropical herb of the ginger family. Can be grown as a container plant in temperate climates, but needs winter protection. Grow in a peat and loam mixture, with added grit or sharp sand. Likes warm moist air conditions. Do not overwater. Root is dried and ground into powder for culinary and medicinal uses.

### Cymbopogon citratus    tropical
**Lemongrass**

Perennial tropical grass with a strong lemon scent that reaches 2–3 ft (60–90 cm) in the greenhouse. Grow in pots from offshoots or seed. Use peat and loam mixture, with added grit or sharp sand to provide good drainage. Do not overwater. Likes consistently warm conditions; reduce watering or do not water at all if it is overcast or raining for any length of time. Used in Asian cooking.

### Dianthus species    Z: 5–8
**Pinks**

Height varies from 8 in (15 cm) to 24 in (60 cm), depending on species. Grow from softwood cuttings in spring or heel cuttings in late summer. Some older cultivars have to be propagated directly after flowering; they may also be divided then. Grow in full sun in well-drained poor soil; most pinks also make good rock-garden plants. Petals have culinary and medicinal uses; dried petals are included in scented sachets.

### Echinacea purpurea    Z: 3–10
**Echinacea, purple coneflower**

Hardy perennial that grows to 4 ft (1.2 m). Sow seed in early spring in a plug tray in greenhouse or propagator, or divide existing plants (in fall or spring) and plant in bed or herb garden. Grow in well-drained soil that will retain a bit of moisture in full sun. Echinacea seems to boost the immune system, thereby helping the body to fight infection, and is used extensively in the pharmaceutical industry. There are several good ornamental cultivars.

### Eruca versicaria    annual
**Arugula**

Half-hardy annual with a height of 2–3 ft (60–90 cm) in flower. Leaves are oval or lance-shaped; flowers are whitish with darker veining. Sow seed from spring on in partial shade in moisture-retentive soil. Sow in fall for winter salads. Cover with a cloche in severe weather. Hard frost and snow will kill arugula, but in mild areas it can be harvested for most of the winter. Adds peppery vigor to salads and cold dishes.

### Eucalyptus citriodora    Z: 9–10
**Eucalyptus**

Tender evergreen tree. Can grow to more than 100 ft (30 m) in its native habitat. A good scented conservatory plant that can be taken outside to a sheltered patio. Sow seed in winter or spring. If kept in pots, feed during growing season. Used in cosmetics and pharmaceuticals.

### Foeniculum vulgare    Z: 4–10
**Fennel**

Growing to 7 ft (2.1 m) in height, with a spread of 18 in (45 cm), this short-lived perennial is best sown straight into a permanent site. Cultivated for its culinary and medicinal purposes, fennel, especially the bronze form, is also a useful ornamental; its yellow flowers are carried in umbels in summer.

### Fragaria vesca    Z: 5–9
**Wild strawberry**

Hardy perennial with a height of 6–12 in (15–30 cm). Leaves are divided into heavily serrated leaflets. White-petaled flowers and sweet, scented fruit that may be red or white. Sow seed in late winter or early spring in pots in the greenhouse, or divide existing plants after fruiting. Grow in fertile moist soil in full sun or part shade.

### Galium odoratum    Z: 3–9
syn. **Asperula odorata**
**Sweet woodruff**

Hardy perennial. Grows to 8 in (20 cm) in flower and has an indefinite spread. Whole plant is aromatic. Leaves are mid-green in whorls. Star-shaped white blooms appear in late spring

or early summer. A plant for deep shade. Sow seed or propagate from root cuttings at almost any time, but the best time is after flowering; cut back and take small pieces of root to plant in pots or cuttings bed in part shade; water after planting. It will soon reshoot. Grows best in alkaline soil under deciduous shrubs and trees. Woodruff jelly is a delicacy in some parts of Europe.

### Helichrysum italicum    Z: 8–9
**Curry plant**

Hardy evergreen perennial that grows to 24 in (60 cm) with a spread of up to 3 ft (1 m). Leaves are narrow and silver-felted; yellow button flowers appear in summer. The whole plant has a strong curry scent. Not much used in the kitchen, rather as an ornamental in gardens. Increase by cuttings in spring or fall. Plant in well-drained soil in full sun. Prolonged wet combined with cold can kill the plant, so, in parts of the country where winters are cold and wet, grow in a large container or overwinter in a cold greenhouse.

### Humulus lupulus    Z: 3–8
**Hops**

Hardy perennial herbaceous climber. Grows to 20 ft (6 m). Has male and female flowers on separate plants. Young leaves are heart-shaped; older leaves have three to five lobes. Whole plant is covered with tiny hooks. Sow in fall in pots and overwinter in a cold frame. Take cuttings or divide female plants in spring or early summer. The golden form of hop is a showy ornamental and can be used in the same way as green hops.

*Hyssopus officinalis*   Z: 3–9
**Hyssop**

Hardy semi-evergreen perennial that grows to a height of 32 in (80 cm) when in flower. Leaves are narrow and aromatic; flowers are blue, pink, or white, depending on variety. Rock hyssop, *H.o.* ssp. *aristatus*, is a good rock-garden or potted plant with dark-blue flowers. Grow in well-drained average soil in full sun. In pots it may need a feed boost if grown in the same soil for several years. Sow seed in plug trays in heated propagator in spring. Cuttings can be taken in late spring and early summer from non-flowering shoots. Seed can also be sown straight into the ground. Thin out if grown as a hedge. Culinary and medicinal plant; use medicinally only on expert advice.

*Juniperus communis*   Z: 2–8
**Juniper**

Slow-growing hardy evergreen shrub or tree that reaches 25 ft (4 m) in height. Needle-like narrow leaves with sharp-pointed tips. Whole plant is aromatic. Sow seed in fall in pots and overwinter in cold frame or cold greenhouse. Take cuttings in spring or fall. Do not use juniper berries during pregnancy or if you suffer from kidney problems.

*Laurus nobilis*   Z: 8–10
**Bay**

Tree or small shrub that grows to 26 ft (8 m), with a spread of 20 ft 3 m) or more. Buy as a well-grown ornamental and use surplus leaves for *bouquet garni* or to flavor oil or vinegar. Pick leaves straight from tree or keep a few dried in a covered jar.

*Lavandula* species   Z: 5–10*
**Lavender**

Hardy or half-hardy evergreen perennials. Vary in height, according to species or cultivar, from 12 in (30 cm) to 36 in (90 cm). One of the most popular plants in the modern garden. All species like an open sunny position in fertile well-drained soil. Seed can be sown in fall or spring in pots or trays; overwinter fall-sown seed in cold greenhouse. Seed, except that from *L. stoechas*, is variable. Cut back plants after flowering, and for a neat bush trim again in spring. Leaves are all very narrow; flower spikes are usually mauve/purple, pale blue or dark blue. Culinary and medicinal herb that is also used in distilled form in cosmetics.

*Levisticum officinale*   Z: 5–8
**Lovage**

Hardy perennial. Grows to 6 ft (2 m) with a spread of up to 3 ft (1 m) or more. Grow in rich, moist, well-drained soil in full sun or part shade; sow seed in fall outside, or in spring in pots in a propagator. Use young leaves in soups and salads; the flavor is better before flowering. Do not take during pregnancy or if you have kidney problems.

*Lonicera* species   Z: 4–11*
**Honeysuckle**

*L. periclymenum* is a deciduous perennial that grows up to 23 ft (7 m). Its fragrant flowers with a pink/red blush are followed by (poisonous) red berries. *L. japonica* is a semi-evergreen deciduous perennial with a height of up to 30 ft (10 m); pale cream flowers turn yellow with age and

are followed by black berries (also poisonous). Sow seed in fall in pots to overwinter outside or in cold frame. Take cuttings in summer or layer at any time. Will grow in sun or part shade in most soils.

*Malva sylvestris*   Z: 4–9
**Mallow**

Biennial or short-lived perennial that, depending on variety, grows to 5 ft (1.5 m). Rounded leaves on basal rosette resemble those of *Alchemilla mollis*, and those that grow up the stem are finely cut or ivy-shaped. Mallows will tolerate most soils, but in overly moist may need staking. Fertile soil in sun or part shade will suit the plants best. Sow seed in fall and overwinter in cold frame, or sow in spring in cool greenhouse. Seed can also be sown in the garden where the plants are to flower. Used in cooking.

*Melissa officinalis*   Z: 4–9
**Lemon balm**

Hardy perennial that grows to 32 in (80 cm). The golden form, *M. o.* 'All Gold,' may need some protection in winter, so mulch with foliage and keep this in place with a cloche. Keep 'All Gold' out of full sun or it will scorch. Golden and variegated forms are fine ornamentals; all are good bee plants. Increase by cuttings or division in fall or spring. Loses its lemon fragrance when cooked, so use fresh in the kitchen.

*Mentha*   Z: 4–11*
**Mint**

Grows to various heights depending on species; some are prostrate. Mint has spreading root runners and can be

very invasive. The leaves of different species have different aromatic qualities. Most mint grows best in part or full shade and need to be restrained to prevent them from taking over whole beds. Cut back in midsummer to rejuvenate plants. Culinary and medicinal herb. Mint oil may cause an allergic reaction and must not be used on babies.

*Monarda didyma*   Z: 4–10
**Bee balm, bergamot, oswego tea**

Hardy perennial that, depending on species or cultivar, grows to between 30 in (75 cm) and 36 in (90 cm), with a spread of 18 in (45 cm). Leaves are elliptical, sometimes toothed, with pointed tips. Flowers are in whorls; colors include pale purple, red, white, soft pink, and purple. All cultivars have to be increased by division or cuttings. Seed from species should be sown in pots or trays. Grow in part shade in moist rich soil; in moisture-retentive soil it will grow in full sun. Mainly grown in perennial flowerbeds for its flowers, but also has culinary and medicinal uses.

*Myrrhis odorata*   Z: 3–7
**Sweet cicely**

Hardy perennial that grows to between 2 ft (60 cm) and 3 ft (90 cm) in flower. Leaves are fernlike; small white flowers in large umbels. Sow seed in pots and overwinter in a cold frame because seeds need stratifying. Root cuttings can be taken in spring or fall, and plants can be divided in spring. For best results, grow in well-drained poor soil. Cut back flower heads before they set seed.

**Hyssopus officinalis**  Hyssop

**Monarda didyma**  Bergamot

**Oenothera biennis**  Evening primrose

***Myrtus communis***   *Z: 9–10*
**Myrtle**

Half-hardy evergreen shrub that grows to 10 ft (3 m). All parts are aromatic. In areas with cold wet winters and prolonged frosts, grow in pots and overwinter in a greenhouse or conservatory. In milder areas, simply protect from too much winter rain. Grow in well-drained soil in full sun. If grown in pots, add sand and bark to loam-based soil. Take softwood cuttings in spring and semi-ripe cuttings in late summer.

***Ocimum basilicum***   *annual*
**Basil**

In temperate northern areas basil is best pot-grown, reaching 18 in (45 cm) with a spread of up to 12 in (30 cm). In warmer regions it can grow to twice that size or more, in the ground. Sow seed in spring either in the ground after frost, or in containers placed in a warm greenhouse or under lights. Transplant as soon as the plant is large enough to handle. Take care not to overwater. Wonderful in salads, in pesto sauce, and with pasta.

***Oenothera biennis***   *Z: 5–8*
**Evening primrose**

Hardy biennial that can reach 4 ft (1.2 m). Lance-shaped leaves make a rosette in the first year, and in the second year the flower spike rises with large yellow, evening-scented flowers. Sow seed in spring in pots, trays, or in the place where you want it to grow. Grow in well-drained soil in a sunny position. Self-sows abundantly. Mainly medicinal, but all parts are edible and can be steamed and eaten.

***Origanum vulgare***   *Z: 5–9*
**Oregano, marjoram**

Several species and varieties; most are hardy in light soil and grow to a height and a spread of up to 24 in (60 cm). Species can be grown in spring in pots or *in situ*; soil should be free-draining and alkaline. Will not thrive in waterlogged soils. Best in full sun. Cultivars will not come true from seed and cuttings should be taken in late spring; plants can also be divided in spring. Used extensively in cooking. An infusion in the bath aids relaxation and a few drops of essential oil on the pillow promotes sleep.

***Papaver somniferum***   *annual*
**Opium poppy**

Hardy annual. Grows to 90 cm (36 in). Sow seed in fall for early flowers and seeds, or in spring for later flowering, straight into the ground in a sunny, fertile, well-drained soil. Thin if necessary. Seeds are used in baking and salads. Other parts are used in pharmaceuticals.

***Pelargonium*** species   *tropical*
**Scented pelargoniums**

Half-hardy plants that, depending on variety and species, grow to varying heights, from 12–40 in (30 cm–1 m). Some species can be grown from seed but it is easier to grow them from cuttings, and all cultivars must be grown from cuttings. Take cuttings in summer or fall as plants are being cut back before overwintering in a frost-free site. Grow in full sun in well-drained soil if in the ground. Reduce watering in fall and keep it to a minimum in winter. Essential oils are used in aromatherapy. The scented leaves are sometimes used to flavor cakes and puddings, but should be removed before serving.

***Perilla frutescens***   *annual*
**Perilla**

Tender annual that makes a good ornamental in the flowerbed. Taller purple form can reach 3 ft (90 cm). Leaves slightly resemble a stinging nettle; can also be confused with the "ruffles" type of basil. Start off in greenhouse or under lights. Transplant, and plant out once frosts are over. Grow in light well-drained soil in full sun or light shade. In cold areas grow in pots. Can stand cold a little better than basil, but likes similar treatment.

***Petroselinum crispum***   *Z: 6–9*
**Parsley**

Hardy biennial that grows to 12 in (30 cm), and to 24 in (60 cm) in flower. Greenish-white flowers in second year. Various forms with heavily curled foliage; others with uncurled, flat leaves. All are good for salads and flavoring. Seeds are chewed in some countries as a remedy for bad breath. Also has a medicinal use, but avoid during pregnancy.

***Pimpinella anisum***   *annual*
**Anise**

Half-hardy annual. Grows to 18 in (45 cm) with a spread of 10 in (25 cm). Sow seed in light well-drained soil in a sunny spot when frosts are over. Do not transplant; thin to 8 in (20 cm) apart. Gather seeds on stalks in late summer as they ripen, and dry in paper bags. Seeds used in fruit dishes and Middle Eastern recipes.

**Portulaca oleracea**   *annual*
**Purslane**

Half-hardy annual growing to 6 in (15 cm) with a spread of 12 in (30 cm). Green or golden leaves. Sow in pots for early planting out or in rows in full sun; thin out and use early in season. Mild-flavored leaves are good in salads and complement stronger-flavored herbs and spices.

**Primula vulgaris**   *Z: 5–9*
**Primrose**

Spring-flowering perennial. Height and spread of 6 in (15 cm). Club-shaped leaves grow from basal rosette. Pale-yellow flowers with delicate honey scent grow singly from the rosette. Grows in moist soil in sun or shade and tolerates heavy soils. Start seed in pots in fall. Leave outside in cold frame or grow fresh seed straight after harvest; germination can be erratic. Plants can be divided in fall. Culinary and medicinal uses.

**Rosa** species   *Z: 2–9*
**Rose**

Old-fashioned roses, especially the scented apothecary's rose, *R. gallica* 'Officinalis,' were traditionally used in herb gardens. Lax sprawling growth. Scented petals are used in cosmetics, to flavor food, and in potpourri.

**Rosmarinus officinalis**   *Z: 7–10\**
**Rosemary**

Numerous cultivars, some upright and others prostrate. Prostrate group reaches a height of 12 in (30 cm). The largest rosemary has a height and a spread of up to 6 ft (2 m). *R. officinalis* can be grown from seed, but cultivars need to be propagated from soft or

semi-ripe cuttings in spring or late summer; they can also be layered. Needs well-drained soil and a sunny position. Grows well in containers. Used in the kitchen, medicinally, and in cosmetic preparations, but avoid during pregnancy. Essential oil must not be taken internally.

**Rumex acetosa**   *Z: 4–8*
**Sorrel**

Sorrel and buckler leaf sorrel (*R. scutatus*) are useful garden plants. Buckler leaf sorrel grows to 6–18 in (15–45 cm) with a spread of 5–24 in (12.5–60 cm). French sorrel is a hardy perennial growing to 2–4 ft (60–120 cm) with a spread of 1 ft (30 cm). Sow seed in spring in propagator from February on, or in late spring outside. Can be divided in spring or fall. A good culinary plant; also used in medicine and, with alum as a mordant, makes a yellow or green dye. Contains oxalic acid, making it poisonous in large doses. People with kidney disease, rheumatism, gout, or kidney stones should avoid sorrel.

**Salvia officinalis**   *Z: 5–8*
**Sage**

Height and spread vary, depending on species, up to 3 ft (90 cm) in height and 28 in (70 cm) spread. Purple, golden, and tricolored sages are good ornamentals as well as culinary and medicinal plants. Ideal container plant for a sunny patio. Not all sages are hardy. *S. elegans* (pineapple-scented leaves) needs to be overwintered in frost-free conditions. Grow from cuttings in spring and summer, and replace plants every few years as they

become very woody. Grow in a light free-draining soil in full sun. Dried leaves can be added to potpourri.

**Sambucus nigra**   *Z: 5–9*
**Elder**

Deciduous hardy perennial shrub or tree. Grows to 10–23 ft (3–7 m) with a spread of up to 12 ft (3.5 m). Good ornamental for beds or wild hedgerows. Fruit must be cooked if used in the kitchen. Flowers used to make fritters and elderflower champagne. Traditionally, berries have been made into a cordial for relieving the symptoms of colds and coughs.

**Sanguisorba minor**   *Z: 4–8*
**Salad burnet**

Hardy evergreen perennial. Grows to 8–24 in (20–60 cm) with a spread of 12 in (30 cm). Sow seed in spring or fall; deadhead regularly. Culinary and medicinal herb, underused in the kitchen. Has a slight taste of cucumber and goes well with fish, cheese, and salads, especially in winter, when other herbs may be scarce.

**Saponaria officinalis**   *Z: 2–8*
**Soapwort**

Hardy perennial growing to 3 ft (90 cm) or more. Tumbling lax plant with lance-shaped oval leaves and clusters of single flowers, but 'Rubra Plena' has double flowers that are at first pink and turn red with age. Can be invasive. Sow seed in fall, as soon as ripe, in a cold frame. Plants appear in spring. Germination is sometimes erratic. Rootstock can be divided in fall or early spring. It has been used medicinally, in cosmetics and as an ingredient of soap.

**Rosa 'Moonlight'** Rose

**Saponaria officinalis** Soapwort

**Tropaeoleum majus** Nasturtium

***Satureja hortensis***    annual
**Summer savory, bean herb**

Half-hardy annual that in flower reaches 12 in (30 cm) with a spread of 8 in (20 cm). Grows bushier if growing tips are harvested often. Sow seed outside when frosts are over, or sow in pots and transplant when soil warms up. Whole plant is aromatic. Use leaves before white or mauve flowers appear. Dries well, and is sold dried. In parts of Europe it is used in almost every dish that incorporates beans.

***Satureja montana***    Z: 5–8
**Winter savory, mountain savory**

Semi-evergreen hardy perennial that grows to 12 in (30 cm) with a spread of 12 in (30 cm) or more depending on conditions. Narrow, lance-shaped leaves; white flowers. Whole plant is very aromatic. Likes full sun and well-drained poor soil. Good ornamental in the right soil; suitable in rock gardens. Take cuttings in spring, or sow seed under lights or in greenhouse in early spring. Seed needs light to germinate. In areas of high rainfall and heavy soil, overwinter some plants in pots, where watering can be minimized. Used to flavor soups, game, and other meats.

***Sesamum indicum***    annual
**Sesame**

Annual tropical herb that grows to 2–3 ft (60–90 cm). Needs long hot summers to produce its nutty seeds. Collect seeds as they ripen before the capsules burst open. Sow after frost danger is past. In cool areas grow under cover. Start in pots with a heated propagation mat to extend growing season. Leaves and seeds used in cooking.

***Symphytum officinale***    Z: 4–9
**Comfrey**

Hardy perennial growing to 3 ft (1 m). Lance-shaped bristly leaves; depending on species or cultivar, flowers can be cream, yellow, blue purple, pink, or red. Sow seed in spring in garden; germination is erratic. Root cuttings or divisions produce plants more quickly. Grow in full sun or part shade; does best in deep moist soil. Used in organic gardening as green manure.

***Tanacetum parthenium***    Z: 4–9
**Feverfew**

Hardy short-lived perennial. Height varies from 2 ft (60 cm) to 4 ft (120 cm); sometimes smaller, especially golden feverfew, *T.p.* 'Aureum,' which reaches 18 in (45 cm) in flower. Grow in rich soil in full sun. Deadhead often. Sow seed in spring or early fall; overwinter plants from fall sowing in cold frame or heated greenhouse. Used to relieve migraines but side effects can be unpleasant.

***Taraxacum officinale***    Z: 3–10
**Dandelion**

Hardy perennial. Height in flower about 10 in (25 cm). Long, deeply toothed leaves grow from basal rosette; flowers are deep yellow. Sow seed in spring in pots or straight into soil. Root cuttings can also be taken. Leaves are added to salads; before use, cover plants for a few weeks so they are blanched and less bitter.

***Thymus*** species    Z: 4–9
**Thyme**

Numerous species, some upright, others creeping. Creeping thymes reach about 1 in (2.5 cm) with a spread of 8 in (20 cm) or more. Shrubby thymes reach 12 in (30 cm) with a spread of 8 in (20 cm). Creeping thymes are useful as ground cover or for scented lawns in full sun. Seed of species can be sown on top of sandy soil. Cultivars are increased only by cuttings; creeping thymes can be increased by division. Deadhead after flowering. The plant is safely eaten in a many dishes, but the oil should be used only on medical advice. Avoid during pregnancy.

***Tropaeoleum majus***    annual
**Nasturtium**

Half-hardy annual. Many cultivated forms that creep or are bushy, so height and spread can vary. Height is usually 8-12 in (20–30 cm), and spread can be 40 in (1 meter) or more. *T. m.* 'Alaska' has variegated leaves and yellow, orange or red flowers. Good plant for a sunny yard and well-drained poor soil. If too well fed, flower production suffers. Sow early in containers, or *in situ* when danger of frost is past. Deadhead regularly. Use young flowers in salads. Seeds, flowers, and leaves are all edible, but treat with caution.

***Urtica dioica***    Z: 3–10
**Nettle**

Hardy perennial that grows to 5 ft (1.5 m); the flowering tops can be even taller in good soil. Leaves are arrow-shaped and deeply serrated, with bristles that break off when touched. Grows in any soil in sun or shade. Roots can also be divided and replanted. A good butterfly plant. Used medicinally, in cooking, in organic gardening, and as a dye plant.

***Verbena officinalis***    Z: 4–8
**Vervain**

Hardy perennial growing to 24-36 in (60–90 cm) when in flower. Leaves are deeply lobed; flowers pale lilac. Sow seed in spring in pots or straight into soil. Grows in any well-drained soil in full sun. Divide existing plants in spring or fall. Avoid during pregnancy.

***Viola odorata***    Z: 6–9
**Violet**

Hardy perennial that can reach 8 in (20 cm), depending on species. Leaves, usually heart-shaped; grow from basal rosette. Scented flowers in a range of colors; dog violet and wood violet have blue or lilac flowers. Sow seed as soon as it ripens in fall and overwinter in a cold frame. Divide or take cuttings from cultivars or a good plant of a species in spring. Grows in moderately heavy fertile soil. Flowers can be used in herbal sachets and perfumes.

***Viola tricolor***    Z: 4–9
**Johnny-jump-up, heartsease**

Hardy perennial that is often grown as an annual. Grows to 12 in (30 cm). Scalloped mid-green leaves; tricolored "little face" flowers. Sow seed in spring in cold frame. Grows in most soils in sun or part shade. Culinary and medicinal herb.

***Zingiber officinale***    Z: 9–11
**Ginger**

Perennial tropical herb. Grown in a container from a division of its rhizome. Requires peat and loam mixture with added sharp sand. Water freely in hot summer months; reduce watering toward winter. Widely used in eastern cuisines.

# suppliers

## SUPPLIERS OF PLANTS & SEEDS

**Avant Gardens**
710 High Hill Road
North Dartmouth
MA 02747-1363
(508) 998-8819
www.avantgardensNE.com

**The Banana Tree Inc.**
715 Northampton Street
Easton
PA 18042
(610) 253-9589
www.banana-tree.com

**Bluestone Perennials**
7211 Middle Ridge Road
Madison
OH 44057-3096
(800) 852-5243
www.bluestoneperennials.com

**W. Atlee Burpee Seed Co.**
300 Park Avenue
Warminster
PA 18974
(800) 888-1447
www.burpee.com

**Carroll Gardens**
444 E. Main Street
Westminster
MD 21157
(800) 638-6334
www.carrollgardens.com

**Catnip Acres Herb Farm**
67 Christian Street
Oxford
CT 06478
(203) 888-5649
www.catnipacres.com

**Companion Plants**
7247 N. Collville Ridge Road
Athens
OH 45701
(740) 592-4643
www.companionplants.com

**The Cook's Garden**
P.O. Box 535
Londonderry
VT 05148
(800) 547-9703
www. cooksgarden.com

**DeBaggio Herbs**
Catalog Dept.
43494 Mountain View Drive
Chantilly
VA 20152
(703) 327-6976
www.debaggioherbs.com

**Filaree Farm**
182 Conconully Hwy
Okanogan
WA 98840
(509) 422 6940
www.filareefarm.com

**Glasshouse Works**
P.O. Box 97
Church Street
Stewart
OH 45778-0097
(800) 837-2142
www.rareplants.com

**Goodwin Creek Gardens**
P.O. Box 83
Williams
OR 97544
(800) 846-7359
www.goodwincreekgardens.com

**Gurney's Seed & Nursery Co.**
110 Capitol Street
Yankton
SD 57079
(800) 806-1972
www.gurneys.com

**Harris Seeds**
355 Paul Road
P.O. Box 24966
Rochester
NY 14624
(800) 514-4441
www.harrisseeds.com

**Heronswood Nursery**
7530 NE 288th Street
Kingston
WA 98346
(360) 297-4172
www.heronswood.com

**Johnny's Selected Seeds**
Foss Hill Road, RR 1
Box 2580
Albion
ME 04910
(207) 437-4301
www.johnnyseeds.com

**Logee's Greenhouses**
141 North Street
Danielson
CT 06239
(888) 330-8038
www.logees.com

**Mellinger's Inc.**
2310 W. South Range Road
North Lima
OH 44452
(800) 321-7444
www.mellingers.com

**Nichols Garden Nursery**
1190 Old Salem Road NE
Albany
OR 97321
(541) 928-9280
www.nicholsgardennursery.com

**Park Seed**
1 Parkton Avenue
Greenwood
SC 29647
(800) 845-3369
www.parkseed.com

**Peaceful Valley Farm Supply**
P.O. Box 2209
Grass Valley
CA 95945
(888) 784-1722
www.groworganic.com

**Piedmont Plant Company**
807 N. Washington Street
P.O. Box 424
Albany
GA 31702
(800) 541-5185
www.plantfields.com

**Redwood City Seed Company**
Box 361
Redwood City
CA 94064
(650) 325-7333
www.redwoodcityseed.com

**Sandy Mush Herb Nursery**
316 Surrett Cove Rd
Leicester
NC 28748
(828) 683-2014

**Seeds of Change**
P.O. Box 15700
Santa Fe
NM 87506
(888) 762-7333
www.seedsofchange.com

**Select Seeds**
180 Stickney Hill Road
Union
CT 06076
(860) 684-9310
www.selectseeds.com

**Shepherd's Garden Seeds**
30 Irene Street
Torrington
CT 06790
(860) 482-0532
www.shepherdseeds.com

**Stokes**
P.O. Box 548
Buffalo
NY 14240
(800) 396-9238
www.stokeseeds.com

**Territorial Seed Company**
P.O. Box 158
Cottage Grove
OR 97424
(541) 942-9547
www.territorialseed.com

**The Thyme Garden**
20546 Alsea Highway
Alsea
OR 97324
(541) 487-8671
www.thymegarden.com

**Tinmouth Channel Farm**
P.O. Box 428 B
Tinmouth
VT 05773
(802) 446-2812

**Wayside Gardens**
1 Garden Lane
Hodges
SC 29695-0001
(800) 845-1124
www.waysidegardens.com

**White Flower Farm**
P.O. Box 50
Litchfield
CT 06759
(800) 503-9624
www.whiteflowerfarm.com

## CRAFT SUPPLIERS

**Glenbrook Farms
Herbs & Such**
15922 76th Street
Live Oak
FL 32060
(888)716-7627
www.glenbrookfarm.com

**Martha By Mail**
P.O. Box 60060
Tampa
FL 33660-0060
(800) 950-7130
www.marthabymail.com

**San Francisco Herb Co.**
250 14th Street
San Francisco
CA 94103
(800) 227-4530
www.sfherb.com

**Target Stores**
33 South Sixth Street
Minneapolis
MN 55402
(888) 304-4000
www.target.com

## NATIONAL ASSOCIATION

**The Herb Society
of America**
9019 Kirtland Chardon Road
Kirtland
Ohio 44094
(440) 256-0514
www.herbsociety.org

---

**KEY TO HARDINESS ZONES**

Except in the case of annual and tropical plants, hardiness zones are indicated in the A–Z of Herbs (pages 116–123). Keep in mind that these are guidelines, not absolutes. Extreme heat, cold or wetness can affect a plant's survival in a given zone.

Zones are based on the average annual minimum temperature for each zone; the smaller number indicates the most northerly zone a plant can survive in; the higher number the most southerly zone the plant will tolerate.

**Z1**  below −50°F (−45°C)
**Z2**  −50° to −40°F (−45° to −40°C)
**Z3**  −40° to −30°F (−40° to −34°C)
**Z4**  −30° to −20°F (−34° to −29°C)
**Z5**  −20° to −10°F (−29° to −23°C)
**Z6**  −10° to 0°F (−23° to −18°C)
**Z7**  0° to 10°F (−18° to −12°C)
**Z8**  10° to 20°F (−12° to −7°C)
**Z9**  20° to 30°F (−7° to −1°C)
**Z10**  30° to 40°F (−1° to 4°C)
**Z11**  above 40°F (4°C)

*An asterisk against an entry in the A-Z of Herbs indicates that zones of hardiness vary according to species.

# index

# Picture credits and acknowledgments

**a** = above, **b** = below, **l** = left, **r** = right, **c** = centre

**1 & 3 l** Linda Garman's home in London; **4–5 top row l & c**; **32–35** Rosemary Titterington at Iden Croft Herbs, Staplehurst, Kent; **36 a, 37 & 39** Rosemary Titterington at Iden Croft Herbs, Staplehurst, Kent; **40–41** Bruisyard Vineyard & Herb Centre, Bruisyard, Suffolk (+44 1728 638281); **41 a** Rosemary Titterington at Iden Croft Herbs, Staplehurst, Kent; **41 b** photograph © Jonathan Buckley; **42–43** Merryweather's Herbs in Herstmonceux, East Sussex; **46** Rosemary Titterington at Iden Croft Herbs, Staplehurst, Kent; **47 & 48** Bruisyard Vineyard & Herb Centre, Bruisyard, Suffolk (+44 1728 638281); **49** Rosemary Titterington at Iden Croft Herbs, Staplehurst, Kent; **52–53** Bruisyard Vineyard & Herb Centre, Bruisyard, Suffolk (+44 1728 638281); **56–57** Linda Garman's home in London; **58 a** Rosanna Dickinson's home in London; **58 b & 59** Mary MacCarthy's house in Norfolk; **60–61** Rosanna Dickinson's home in London; **64 & 65 l** Linda Garman's home in London; **66–67** Linda Garman's home in London; **68** Mary MacCarthy's house in Norfolk; **70 r & 76 a** Linda Garman's home in London; **76 b, 77 & 80 l** Mary MacCarthy's house in Norfolk; **80 r** Linda Garman's home in London; **81** Mary MacCarthy's house in Norfolk; **85 & 128** Rosanna Dickinson's home in London.

The publishers give special thanks to David Grist, the U.S. consultant.

Barbara Segall would like to thank Gisela Mirwis for her research.

Rose Hammick would like to thank Carol Hammick and Adam Tindle for the use of the glasshouse and vegetable garden, Claire Farrow and William Morris, Zosia at White and Gray, Victoria Robinson, Amanda and Sarah Vesey, Georgina Hammick, Katie Rudaz, Richard Mole, Charlotte Packer, Clementine Young and Ashley Western.

**The publishers would like to thank the following organizations for providing information and photographic locations:**

**Bruisyard Vineyard & Herb Centre**
Church Road, Bruisyard
Saxmundham, Suffolk IP17 2EF
+44 1728 638281
*The 4 hectare (10 acre) site incorporates a vineyard, a winery, a herb garden, a water garden, a children's play area and a picnic area. Producers of award-winning Bruisyard English wines and a wide selection of herbs.*
Pages **40–41, 47, 48, 52–53**.

**Iden Croft Herbs**
Staplehurst, Kent
+44 1580 891432
www.herbs-uk.com
*Plants, seeds and garden visits. Themed show gardens include culinary, medicinal, patio, potpourri and cottage gardens.*
Pages **32–35, 36 a, 37, 39, 41 a 46, 49**.

**Mary MacCarthy**
+44 1328 730133
*Decorative paintwork and murals.*
Pages **58 b, 59, 68, 76 b, 77, 80 l, 81**.

**Merryweather's Herbs**
Merryweather's Farm, Chilsham Lane
Herstmonceux, East Sussex BN27 4QH
+44 1323 833316
*Owners Ian & Liz O'Halloran. A unique project creating 2.2 hectares (5½ acres) of gardens and wildlife habitat and incorporating a small nursery.*
Pages **42–43**.